MOVING ON
SHORT STORY TO NOVEL

MOVING ON
SHORT STORY TO NOVEL

A STEP-BY-STEP GUIDE

Della Galton

Published by Accent Press Ltd – 2012
ISBN 9781908192417

Printed and boundby CPI Group (UK) Ltd, Croydon, CR0 4YY

Cover design by Red Dot Design

For Ian Burton, who taught me everything I know about writing, and Nancy Henshaw, a writer I very much admire.

Acknowledgements

As always I'd like to thank all at Accent Press for their amazing support and encouragement. Thank you to the writers who gave me quotes for the Tips from the Experts section at the end. Thank you also to every writer I have ever spoken to for their insight and their wisdom. Being part of a writing fellowship is amazing.

Foreword

The difference between writing a short story and a novel is viewed by some as similar to the difference between a snack and a meal, or a sprint and a marathon. With the shorter work, the end is almost within sight, a target one can almost visualise; with a novel, it allows for greater expansion, a host of characters and plenty of scope for description, plot, dialogue and drama.

Jumping 'up' from short fiction to a novel is most often a question of greater scale and stamina; a writer accustomed to creating short fiction, for example, might be disciplined to working to a tight schedule of, say, 2,000 words, where every single word counts. Descriptive narrative in a short story does not always allow the full run of words one might wish to use, and suddenly writing to a much wider scope, with room to expand far more than one is used to, can be a touch of freedom too far.

And some short stories should remain just that: short stories, rather than becoming longer stories in short pants which suddenly run out of wind.

(Conversely, it has to be said, some writers accustomed to working on a very broad canvas, say, 90,000 words, can just as easily find themselves daunted by the severe constraints of working to a 2,000 word maximum, a skill in itself, which probably equals only half a chapter in their normal line of work.)

But it can be done, as many writers have found. And the jump from short story writer to novelist shouldn't stop anybody trying. The main advice for someone wishing to make the transition between the two might be to proceed with careful planning, and an understanding of what is required.

Della Galton's *Moving On – Short Story To Novel* will help you do that. Packed with examples, this step-by-step guide will demonstrate the approaches to writing long fiction versus short; the differences between short-story ideas and novel ideas; of developing plot, character and setting in the two entirely different mediums; of introducing a character in a short story compared with a novel; of the scope of dialogue in the two mediums ... not to mention a host of other things which you probably hadn't even thought about.

A must for writers wanting to make the transition from short fiction to novels, this guide is also useful to novelists wishing to embark on short story writing.

Written in Della's usual down-to-earth, informal manner, this book demonstrates that, above all, size does matter!

Adrian Magson
Crime/spy thriller author and writer
www.adrianmagson.com

CONTENTS

INTRODUCTION

Introduction

I began my writing career with short stories, as many writers do. I remember being told by my tutor at the time that short stories were a good place to start. I could learn the skills and techniques of creative writing, and, if ever I wanted to write something longer, having a background of short story writing would stand me in good stead.

I think she was right. It's as true today as it ever was that whatever writing you do, whether it's writing letters, non-fiction, a blog, or even writing a personal diary, the act of putting words on paper will help you to hone and develop your skills.

Apart from one amateurish attempt at a novel when I was in my early twenties it was several years before I decided to have a go at writing full-length fiction. I found, like several other writers I have since spoken to, that while my tutor was right in many respects, there are a lot of differences.

Writing a novel was not just about, as I had once thought, producing more words! Although that is, of course, one of the things you have to do. There are several other differences.

This book is about looking at those differences in detail and helping you to work out how to make the transition between short and long fiction.

Chapter One

What's the difference between writing a short story and a novel?

I'm going to spend the rest of this book answering this question in some depth, but I thought it might be helpful to very briefly outline some of the differences in Chapter One. After that you'll need to go to the relevant section of the book to see how these differences actually work out in practice.

Length

Length is probably the most obvious difference. Not many short stories are longer than about 5,000 words and even a short novel, for example a category romance, is at least ten times longer than that. The average length for a novel, if there is such a thing, is somewhere between about 70,000 and 120,000 words, depending on the type of novel and the publisher's requirements.

So setting out to write one is not a five-minute job. Unlike a short story, which can be written and edited in a few days, a novel is going to take a substantial amount of time and work.

Timescale

Generally in a short story the timescale is short, an hour,

an afternoon, or a week. If you try to cover too much time in a short story it will end up reading like a synopsis. A short story is a glance at a group of characters. A novel is a good long look at them.

Some novels may only cover an afternoon, or a day, or a week, but we will get to know the characters in depth in this time. And generally a novel will cover more time than this. Some novels, notably sagas, follow characters through their entire lifetime.

Idea

There is a difference between ideas for short stories and ideas for novels. If you have been writing for a while, or even if you haven't, you'll probably be able to spot which ideas are more suitable for short stories and which are more suitable for novels and where the crossover is between the two.

It is also possible to use some ideas for both short stories and novels, but the treatment and development of them will not be the same.

Planning and plotting

A short story plot, by its nature, needs to be kept fairly simple. There isn't enough room for it to be complicated. Generally, a short story will tend to focus on a single event or theme. It is possible to sit down and begin a short story having done little or no planning.

A novel will need much more plot than a short story, or perhaps one main plot and some interlinking subplots to sustain the length. Whereas a short story can follow a single idea, longer fiction tends to need more than one.

I am reluctant to say that it's impossible to sit down

and begin your novel having done little or no planning, but I have tried it and discovered to my cost that it is not necessarily the best idea.

Setting

Setting is important in both short stories and novels but in a short story it will be brushstroked in, probably quite sparsely. In a novel it will be much more evident. In certain types of novels, for example regional sagas, setting is equally as important as character. It's also necessary, both in short stories and novels, to show setting through the eyes of your characters. Do not paste it into your story in blocks or your readers will probably skip it!

Characters

A short story of one or two thousand words almost certainly won't have more than two or three characters, one of whom will be the main character. There is a lot more room for characters in a novel although that doesn't mean you should attempt to have a cast of hundreds! You will still need to know whose story it is and all of your characters must be essential to the plot.

The difference between characters in a short story and characters in a novel is development. We will look in detail at the differences between developing a short story character and a novel character in Chapter Five.

Viewpoint

In a short story there is often (although not necessarily) the room for only one viewpoint. In a novel there is room for more. Using the viewpoint of more than one character can add a great deal of depth. Equally, you can stay in one viewpoint in a novel. If anything, it's possibly harder to stay in one viewpoint in a novel because the story can only unfold via what the viewpoint character, i.e. the character that has the viewpoint, sees, hears and feels.

You can use the narrative viewpoint in short and long fiction, but in my experience it's best for a new writer to proceed with caution when choosing this route.

Dialogue

Whether you are writing a short story or novel, your characters will need to have individual and recognisable voices. This is a natural progression and isn't as difficult as it sounds if you have developed them sufficiently.

It is actually much easier to give your characters different voices in a novel than it is in a short story, as you'll have more room and time for development on the page. Writers who have taken the trouble to give their characters different voices can reap the rewards when their readers recognise characters just by how they speak. We've all read novels in which the characters are so alive they jump off the page. Giving them good strong voices is one of the ways of achieving this.

Pace

If you're writing a short story of one or two thousand words then you need to hook the reader immediately and plunge straight into the story. There is not much room for scene setting or back story.

In longer fiction you can afford to move at a slower pace. This does not mean you can afford to waffle. Every word must still count. For many short-story writers, pace is the hardest thing to get right when they begin to write longer fiction. Learning to adjust and control pace is, however, essential if you are to make the transition between short and long fiction. Pace is discussed in detail in Chapters Nine, Ten and Eleven.

Structure and flashback

How will you structure your novel? Deciding before you begin to write can help you to plan it. Structure is a short-story writer's friend, but it's a novelist's best friend because there are far more options.

Your novel might have a prologue. It might be split into parts and it will probably have chapters. You're not limited to flashback. You can use flash forward too! It's great fun to play with time in a novel.

The first paragraph and the first page

In my experience, writing the opening paragraph of a short story is a lot easier than writing the end. But in a novel I find the opposite to be true.

In both it's vital to get it right: the beginning of your story is the first thing an editor or competition judge or agent or publisher sees. But there are some differences between writing the opening paragraph of a short story and a novel and these differences get more pronounced as you write the rest of the first page.

I have a personal theory that it's difficult to write the first page of your novel until you've written the rest of it.

The middle

Writing the middle of a short story is relatively

straightforward. It isn't very long and moves swiftly towards the end. Writing the middle of a novel is much harder and is where a lot of first-time novelists fall down. The hundreds, perhaps thousands, of half-finished novels languishing in drawers around the country pay testimony to this fact.

There are some things you can do at the planning stage to make sure the middle of your novel is strong. Middles are discussed in detail in Chapter Ten.

The end

Ending a short story is often the hardest part, I think because you have very little room to create a satisfying ending. Bringing your novel to a satisfying conclusion is a lot easier, fortunately. Ends are explored in more depth in Chapter Eleven.

The title

For me, finding titles is always very difficult, whether they are for short stories or novels, and, although I might have a working title while writing a novel, this is rarely the title of the finished product – for reasons that we'll look at later.

Titles go through fashions whether you are writing short stories or novels. In both cases you won't need a title until you've finished your manuscript, but when you do come to look for one there are a few things to bear in mind. Titles are explored in detail in Chapter Fifteen.

The synopsis

You won't necessarily need one for a short story, but

electronic publishing has changed this a bit, so it's handy to know the difference between a short story synopsis and the type you'd need for a novel. Knowing how to write a synopsis is currently essential for a novelist.

Blurbs

It's becoming increasingly common for short-story editors to ask for blurbs to accompany short stories. If you are writing short stories for emarkets, the blurb is often used to sell the story online. So it's critical for a writer to be able to produce good ones. Your story may even be judged on its blurb. If an editor has seen similar plots before she may not be so interested in reading your story. Beware.

Blurbs are also used to sell novels, they are the piece on the back cover, which most potential buyers will read before making a decision to buy, or not. While an agent or publisher may do them for you, writers are often asked to do this task too, so it's a useful skill to have.

Writing a blurb before you start writing anything else is also a good way of deciding if your idea is a short story or novel idea.

Selling/publishing

Selling a short story is relatively straightforward. You package it up and send it to your intended market, whether it be small press, magazine, or radio. Selling a novel or finding an agent to represent you is slightly more difficult. It might be necessary to also sell yourself – in the nicest possible way, I hasten to add!

Why is it necessary to sell yourself? Well, when you sell a short story to a magazine, the editor simply edits and publishes it and sends you a cheque. If you sell a novel they will probably have to work with you a lot longer and agents and editors tend to be very busy people. Naturally, they will be keen to work with writers who are amenable and pleasant and won't make their life more difficult.

The latter will also apply to writers sending out more than one short story to the same editor.

Rejections

One of the things that stopped me writing a novel was the fear of rejection. It was bad enough when my short stories came flying back with a rejection slip. The prospect of getting a rejection for something that had taken me a year or so to write seemed unbearable. I didn't think I would cope. But I did find ways to cope. I had to because the alternative would have been to give up writing, which was an even more unbearable prospect. I have several tried and tested methods (unfortunately) of coping with rejection for both short stories and novels. I have shared them in Chapter Twenty-three.

Chapter Two
The Idea

What's the difference between a short story idea and a novel idea?

I believe that this is to do with size. Some ideas lend themselves naturally to short stories and some lend themselves to novels. But there are some that would work just as well for both, although of course the treatment would be different. This brings me on to the question that I asked myself when I first began to write novels:

Do I have a big enough idea?

This is tricky to ascertain, but it's important. What exactly is a big idea anyway? What's the difference between a short story idea and a novel idea? Is there even a difference? Surely a romance could be either? Yes, it could. A murder could be either too, couldn't it? Absolutely. We've all read plenty of short stories and novels which have a romance or a murder at their heart. So is there actually a difference at all?

I believe there *is* a difference. But it's probably easier to look at some examples.

Examples of short story ideas and novel ideas

Let's start with some obvious short story ideas. I've

picked out examples from the last few I've sold.

Example One
Pageboy Blues – published in *My Weekly*, 2011

A small boy is told to sit still in the kitchen while his mum and aunt get ready for his aunt's wedding. He's too restless to sit still and when he hears his aunt needs something blue for her wedding, he resolves to find it for her. Unfortunately, the only blue things he can see are the bluebells in the next door neighbour's garden. He jumps over the fence to get one for his aunt, ruining his wedding outfit in the process, not to mention breaking the fence. He is later forgiven, despite not doing what he was told, because his heart was in the right place.

Now, this is a short story idea through and through. Why is that exactly?

The time span is very short. True, but the time span of some novels is short too. The main character is a child. True, but then lots of novels have a child as the main character.

It's really a short story idea because the essential problem is so small. Yes, the character is faced with a problem (not being able to sit still) but it will very quickly be resolved.

Example Two
Hope Cove – published in *The People's Friend,* 2011

A girl, recovering from the death of her father, is taken away by her husband on a weekend break. She realises that life goes on.
This one is slightly trickier. This plot has a bigger idea at

its heart, that is, moving on from grief, which is at the heart of many a novel and indeed at the heart of many a short story. It worked as a 1000-word short story, because we only have a quick glimpse at the problem, and we only ever meet the main character and her husband. We've never known her father and we don't meet her mother or indeed anyone else in her life. We look at one aspect of the character, her recovery from grief, and the part her husband plays in it.

So is it perhaps the number of characters and the development of an idea that determines whether it will be suitable for a short story or a novel? Certainly in short stories you won't usually have more than two, or possibly three main characters.

Example Three
The Colour of Chiffon – published in *Take a Break*, 2011

This story is about a girl, Rainey, who grew up in a fairground, but left to marry a rich businessman. Five years later she realises she's made a mistake, he is controlling and manipulative, and she leaves him in order to find the fair and in doing so to find herself again.

This story was slightly open-ended. The reader doesn't know whether Rainey will find the fair or not, but the reader does know she has found the strength to leave her manipulative husband. Whether she finds the fair again is almost incidental. The main thing is that she has altered as a character and her life has taken an up turn.

Oddly enough, I wrote the original version of this story in 2005 and I then went on to develop it into my second novel, *Helter Skelter*, which was published in 2007. In the original version the main character was called Vanessa. I changed it to Rainey for the story version because they were such totally different characters.

So, who knows, you may have already written the short story which will become your first or second novel! I think the reason this story worked as a novel was because it had enough elements that could be developed. Let's take a quick look at them.

The main character's motivation is to leave her husband and go in search of her past life and her past love. There is a lot of scope here to explore her past. What happened and why did she leave?

Her past is sufficiently interesting (fairground) for there to be plenty of room for development here, too. How did she come to be brought up on a fairground? Where are her parents, who didn't, incidentally, bring her up?

Her husband will do anything to stop her. Indeed, the reader soon discovers that he has already take steps to ensure his wife's past is gone for good. There is a lot of conflict here too.

So, yes, *The Colour of Chiffon*, despite being written as a short story had all the elements necessary to become a novel. Not all short stories will translate. You will need to think about this.

Of course it's often the case that you want to write about a particular theme or subject, for example, grief, or the past, and you just write about one aspect of it in a short story. Whereas in a novel you have the room to explore it in depth.

Is my idea original?

The answer to this is that it's probably not. Are there any

original ideas left on the planet? Perhaps there are, but I haven't found any, and anyway it doesn't matter. Whether you are writing a short story or a novel it is not the originality of the idea that will determine whether it's a success. It is the way you write it. It is your own original treatment of the idea and your voice that will make it sink or swim.

Does my idea have staying power?

When you come up with an idea you think will make a good novel or short story, ask yourself these two questions:

Can I give this idea a sufficiently original treatment or structure to make it fresh and exciting and new? Think *Time Traveller's Wife* by Audrey Niffenegger.

Am I truly passionate about writing this story?

Actually I think that if you can say yes to these two questions then you should proceed. Whether you are writing 1000 words or 90,000 words, being able to bring a new slant and a new passion to an idea is likely to make it successful.

Does my idea fit a genre or market?

If you're writing a short story and you aim to sell it, then your market is pretty critical. Look at your market first, be it magazine or ezine or competition. Then write a story that is aimed squarely at the market.

But perhaps a more pertinent question to ask might be who are my readers? If you want to be read, then you should be considering your readers. But what if you are writing a first novel? Do you have to consider such things then? Can't you just write the novel you've always wanted to write?

I would say yes, but with a conditional clause. Why not write the novel you've always wanted to read. One of the best pieces of advice I was ever given was from a novelist friend.

"Remember we are in the entertainment business," she said with a smile.

That does not mean you have to set out to be hugely entertaining or write a humorous novel, although if you can write humour well, you'll probably get a long way doing exactly this. What it means, or at least what I interpret it to mean, is that you need to write stories (be they long or short) that people will want to read.

The mistake I made when I wrote my first novel, and my first short stories come to that, was to write exactly what I wanted to write about. In the case of my short stories this meant surreal fantasy and stories heavily based on analogies. The latter can work, but selling surreal fantasy is pretty tricky – especially to women's magazines.

My first serious attempt at a novel was way too dark. I quite like writing about black subjects, so I chose incest and murder as the themes for my first novel. Not just any old murder, I hasten to add, but murdering your mother. Hmmm – this was great fun to write, but probably not half as much fun to read.

In fact, I remember the comment of one agent very well. "I could never represent a book with such horrible subject matter." I could almost feel her shudder in the words. And I'm sure she was right.

How do I know if my idea is marketable?

This is a tricky one. I'm not sure it's possible to know this for sure, as virtually any idea can be marketable if it's written in the right way. I believe, and I'm talking about short stories and novels here, that you should write the kind of story you'd love to read, but that you should also have one eye on the market.

If you are writing a story or novel that you don't really want to write, purely as a means to making money (good luck with that!) then it's likely to show in the writing. Your words have a way of becoming less sincere, less believable, and, ironically, you are less likely to sell them. At least this is my experience of writing.

Summary of differences

Short story ideas often feature problems which are resolvable quickly.

Short story ideas focus on one aspect of a character's life, or one aspect of a problem or relationship in their life.

In novels the stakes must be higher. The character's problem must be something that really matters. It doesn't have to be life or death, although it often is.
In a novel, issues tend to be deeper.

A big idea will have depth, which means it will expand in more than one direction, whereas a short story idea can be quite linear.

Chapter Three
Organising Your Writing Time

Space and time to write

You may have the luxury of having all the time in the world to write, but if you're fitting writing around other work or commitments you might want to read this section.

Do I need larger chunks of time to write a novel than a short story?

This might seem like an odd question. Naturally you'll need more time to write a novel, but I find, although you may be different, that I actually need longer stretches of time when I'm writing longer fiction, regardless of the amount of words I'm writing.

Let me explain. When I sit down to write a story I might only have half an hour or an hour allocated to that story. (That doesn't mean I'll finish it in that time, mind you!) But I'm quite happy to start it and write as much as I can in half an hour.

But there is no way I'd contemplate working on my novel if I only had half an hour to spare. I need the security of a stretch of time. I find that novel writing eats up huge swathes of time that short story writing doesn't. This is partly because I edit back a thousand or so words, each time I sit down, so I can get fully into the mood of the chapter I'm writing. But it's also because it's vital to get continuity of voice and my mood might have changed.

For some reason, I don't find continuity a problem when I come back to a short story, however long it is. You might be different, but this is worth bearing in mind.

However, sometimes, you may only have a very short chunk of time in which to write. Here are some ways to maximise the use of your writing time.

Time Saving Tips

Tip number one – know what you're going to write

This might sound obvious but it's surprising how many people don't do this. Don't waste time sitting at your desk thinking. Plan what you will write before you sit down.
If it's a short story it's not a bad idea to have the name of the main character in your head, along with the first line, before you sit down to write.

If it's a novel it's a good plan to know what scene you're going to write next and have an idea of how it will start and what you intend to show about your characters and plot in that scene.

This is partly to save time, but also because starting is the hardest part of writing. You wouldn't believe how long I can prevaricate before I sit down to write.

Tip number two – turn off the internet

In fact, I can prevaricate for quite a long time even when I am sitting down ready to write. Twitter and email and Facebook are very good distractions. So Tip Number Two is to turn off the internet when you sit down to write.

Being connected to the internet is not going to further

your mission of getting words on the page one little bit. It is definitely going to stop you getting words on the page.

Tip number three – research only essentials

I also find it's very tempting to research every little detail of what I'm writing as I go along. This is mainly because I have the internet at my finger tips. In the old days when I was writing a story, or in some cases a novel, I would write notes about things I needed to research as I went along, but I'd do the actual research later. I got a lot more writing done this way. So Tip number three is to do your research later. (So you definitely don't need the internet on. If that was your reason for ignoring Tip number two. Turn it off now!)

In fact, this can save you even more time than you think because some scenes you write will later need to be cut, rendering any research you've already done for them unnecessary.

Writing Frequency

If you write short stories then you can snatch time here and there. If you write fast (and you can type quickly) then you might finish a story in one sitting. This is very useful if you can do it because your mood/state of mind throughout is likely to be the same. You may have been moved to write your story by a particular emotion and you will still be able to feel or recall that emotion when you have completed your first draft. It doesn't matter if you're in a different mood when you edit it. You might edit it a fortnight later, in fact, it's often quite a good idea to let some time elapse and do your editing with a different 'head' on, so to speak.

But novels are a trickier beast. If too much time elapses between you writing one bit and the next everything tends to go stale. It's hard to recapture the mood you were in when you wrote the beginning of a scene if you started it a fortnight ago. For this reason I'm strongly in favour of clearing yourself some regular time if you plan to write a novel. If possible, this should be daily. The less time there is between writing sections of your novel the easier it will be. I think this is one of the reasons *NaNoWriMo* (write a novel in a month – see website below) works so well. *www.nanowrimo.org*.

For one thing the novel will be in your head, constantly in your mind. You might even find yourself dreaming about it. This is no bad thing. You will learn things about the characters and plot 'off page'. I also find it quite helpful to talk through difficult aspects of plot or characters with my long-suffering other half. He talks about his work, which mostly involves fridges (he's a refrigeration engineer) and I talk about what my characters are doing and what their motivations might be and any difficulties I'm having with the plot.

Sometimes, just the very act of talking about the characters will resolve the difficulties. And it also means that we never run out of things to say! He's always fixing fridges, I'm always writing.

Motivation – how do I stay motivated?

Most of us are motivated when we begin writing. We are excited about the idea we've had, be it short story or novel, but it's easy to run out of steam, particularly if things don't go well.

How you keep motivated depends on what type of person you are. I find either of the following works well:

It's a numbers game – short stories

If you are a goal-setting person, set goals. This is exactly what I did when I was planning to give up my day job and write short stories for a living. I wanted to know what percentage of my short stories I sold so I decided to work it out. I devised what I called a 28-week-plan, which was basically a weekly chart I could fill in with the title of my story and the date written and the date sold.

While I was still working full time I would write one short story a week for 28 weeks. I would do this no matter what happened. As I went along I would attempt to sell them and see what percentage I sold. The idea being that I would then know how many stories I needed to write a month to make a living.

I like deadlines so I found this very motivating. Of those 28 stories I sold 19 (67 per cent). I decided I'd like to sell 6 stories a month, and as writing and selling stories isn't an exact art (understatement) I decided I'd better assume my percentage was more like 50 per cent. Therefore I would need to write 12 stories a month (3 a week) in order to make a living.

This probably all sounds very mathematical, and, believe me, I'm no mathematician, but it did work. I suppose you could say that what really motivated me was money. I had to write 3 stories a week in order to make a living.

But actually, what really motivated me was the dream of being a full-time writer. These numbers were only the means by which I could achieve my dream.

It's a numbers game – novels

I do a similar thing when I'm writing a novel. I use

numbers to inspire me. I decide on a time frame for a novel to be completed and then I work backwards to see what I need to do in order to make that happen. For example, if I want to write a 90,000 word novel in three months I will need to write around 1000 words a day. If I want to write it in six months I will need to write around 500 words a day.

I find it incredibly motivating to keep a running total as I go. And I refuse to leave my computer until I've done my allocated number of words.

A word of warning here. There is going to be a lot of editing to do and the words might not be perfect words, but at least they will be written. It's a lot easier to edit and shape novels when they are written. I'm also a firm believer in the fact that nothing you write is ever wasted. Even scenes that you subsequently cut will have helped develop your characters and plot.

Another good way of keeping motivated

Join a writing group or class and commit yourself to reading out your work every week.

"This is fine when it comes to short stories," I hear you shout. "But I'm not reading my 'work in progress' to a group of writers. What if they put me off writing it?"

This is a valid point. Not all novelists like reading out their 'work in progress', although some find it motivating, particularly if a group of writers, or even one writer, is anxiously waiting for the next instalment. I once wrote a whole novel like this.

But even if you don't want to read out your 'work in progress' it does work well with a finished novel.

It's an excellent way to motivate yourself through the editing process. Read out a section, get feedback, and then edit and rewrite before going on to the next section.

Working practices and equipment

Do you work on a computer or use pen and paper? Does it matter? Most households seem to own a computer these days. But actually, I'm not going to say you must have a computer to write – because this is patently not true. You can do it just as well with a paper and pen. (OK, a lot of paper and several pens). Possibly you'll save more time using a computer because it's easier to edit work on a screen than write it all out again. Then again, you may not be able to type in which case you won't save time trying.

Also, if you actually weigh up how much time you waste when you use a computer on things like: learning how it all works; email; Facebook; Twitter; internet shopping and irresistible (not to mention addictive) games you might actually save time using a pen and paper.

However, a computer will come into its own when you have to present your manuscript professionally and send it off. You will need to have your work typed. If you have someone to do this for you, then excellent, if not, you might just need a computer. Or perhaps there's an argument here for buying a dedicated word-processor and printer – if it's still possible to get such a thing. I'm not the most technologically-minded person in the world. I recently bought a new phone and had to consult the manual to work out how to answer it. But I'm beginning to think some kind of electronic notepad might be a more satisfactory arrangement than a computer.

Printers

If you buy a printer and you plan to write novels you will

want to watch your ink consumption. Buying a very cheap printer, which uses very expensive ink cartridges, is false economy. Generally, laser printers are better value for money if you want to print a lot of pages.

Chairs

Also, make sure you have a half-decent chair and don't spend long uninterrupted hours in front of a screen, or hunched over a desk, without taking decent breaks.

I think that actually it's much harder work, physically, writing full-length fiction because writers do tend to get so involved in it that the hours flick by without us noticing. This is very bad for your health.

I developed an RSI-style injury this year, which has made me much more aware of using devices like arm rests for my mouse, and also much more aware of the position in which I sit.

Summary of differences

Time commitment – you are likely to spend longer at your desk when you write novels than short stories, simply because writing novels tends to involve sitting for longer stretches of time. Also, when you are writing novels you can become so deeply immersed that hours flick by unnoticed.

Physical commitment – this may have an impact on your health, not to mention your relationships with your family. There is a good argument here for heading off to a writer's retreat, at least in the early stages of writing a novel.

Financial commitment – buy a printer that is economical to run. This isn't so critical when you're writing short stories, but regularly printing out 100,000 words, either to edit or to send off to publishers on an ink-thirsty printer, is a quick route to bankruptcy!

Chapter Four
Idea to Plot

What's the difference between a novel plot and a short story plot?

I am tempted to say length, but actually, as we've already discovered when we looked at ideas, it is very often breadth and depth. When I first decided to write a novel I didn't fully understand those two things. I thought that to sustain the amount of words a novel required I would simply need to have a lot more things happening.

For example, my first novel, *Passing Shadows*, is about a woman, Maggie, who is coming to terms with her past, and the fact that she's always felt second best. She's had a bad relationship with her late mother, and she finds it difficult to trust. She immerses herself in an animal sanctuary in Wiltshire (animals are safer than people), but love finds her. Naturally it brings its own complications. The man she falls for turns out to be the father of her best friend's child.

Now, bearing in mind that *Passing Shadows* is a romance, this is probably enough plot to be going on with.

But I didn't think so. In my original draft I added in several more conflicts, I had a kidnap and blackmail storyline, an adoptive father storyline. An irate farmer storyline. I ended up with a great big mess of strands, none of which were developed. How could they be? There wasn't room. I might add here that *Passing Shadows* originally started out as a serial, with a word length of around 20,000 words, and I still thought I needed all this plot!

You probably have more sense than this! In which case skip this section. But coming from a short story background, as I had, I genuinely thought more words equalled more plot. And actually I do occasionally read first novels (mostly unpublished) where the writer is obviously under a similar misconception.

Starting with such a major misconception was a big disadvantage for me. I found out via (sometimes quite painful) experience and writing thousands and thousands of words that more words mean more development, nothing else.

This is one of the reasons I'm writing this book. When I started writing novels I wish someone had told me exactly what is meant by developing plot and character. So, what do they mean?

Well, when you're writing a novel you do *not* need a lot more going on. You need a lot more development of the strands you have. This means we need reaction from characters, particularly the main character. We don't need to be swept along in a mad rush with them as they deal with conflict after conflict, such as kidnap and adoption and mad farmers, but we *do* need to know how they feel and how they grow as people, and how the problems they face and have faced affect them and their relationships. It is your character's reactions and feelings and actions that will make the reader care about them. With luck.

A universal premise

In order to explore plot development in a bit more detail,

I'd like to show you an example of a plot, which could work as either a short story or a novel, depending on which aspects are developed.

Here's the premise in a couple of sentences: *A poverty-stricken African boy is asked to find a poacher a rare species of giraffe. He will be well paid for his efforts, but are some things more important than money?*

Here's the story in 742 words. It was published in *My Weekly* under the title, *The Prize*:

The Prize – the short story

"The first one to find me a giraffe with white legs gets money." His eyes glittered in his pale face and a gun gleamed at his belt.

Why a giraffe with white legs? None of us really understood what was at stake. We just wanted to please this stranger. And we wanted money.

My brother, Peter, swatted a fly from his bare leg and stared at the man's shoes, all shiny and brown even in the dust of Nakuru.

"You know where to find giraffe, yeah?"

"Sure." I spoke for us all. I was the oldest. "How many you want?"

The hunter bared his teeth in a smile. "One'll do." He wriggled his fingers at his head. "Special giraffe with five horns and white legs?" He rustled notes, more money than I had ever seen. "You get giraffe with five horns, I give you money – we have deal, yeah?"

"We have deal." His hand closed over mine. His skin felt cool and smooth and when I took my hand away, his strange foreign smell was on my fingers.

"Go on then, Mowgli, get on with it."

There was something mocking in his voice, but I didn't care. By nightfall I would have money, which meant I'd no longer have the aching space in my belly, but more importantly Mother would be relieved.

It was relief I saw in her eyes most. A weary relief, as though she was pleased she'd got through another day. I don't remember seeing that look when I was younger – maybe it was because things weren't as bad then.

My aunt Lisnet had died of the sickness. Mother had nursed her until the end. Aunt Lisnet, who had once been taller than mother, so graceful and proud and always smiling, had faded away on the bare earth floor of our house, her face all hollowed out and her arms like black matchsticks.

Now there were my cousins to feed too, we needed money like never before.

These thoughts swirled in my head as I ran through the bush, looking for fresh dung, feeling the heat of the day rising up from the earth. I knew a herd had passed recently, Peter and I had seen them on our way back from school.

There were lots of giraffe in the park, but not many of the type the man wanted. Rothschild's were rare, an endangered species, protected from poachers by the wardens.

It was around sunset that I found her. I don't know what instinct led me to the clearing, but there she was – my prize. She swayed into view in that curiously graceful blunder of giraffes. I wondered why she hadn't gone on with the others. Why she'd waited, almost invisible against the trees. Then I saw the smaller shadow behind her, the calf doddery in her wake, its skin still damp from birth.

I held my breath. I had never seen anything so impossibly fragile, so beautiful.

The giraffe and I were so close I could see the dark fear in her eyes. I was surprised she hadn't attacked. Maybe she was too weak from the delivery.

She would be an easy prize. I pictured the relief on my mother's face. I thought of how long the money could make that relief last.

I thought of Aunt Lisnet coughing and pleading with my mother, "Look after my babies." She'd had fear in her voice – as though she knew she couldn't hold on much longer.

I looked back at the giraffe. It was difficult to meet her eyes. But I couldn't afford sentimentality. My family were desperate.

Warily I backed out of the clearing. I could hear the crashing of hunters' feet still some distance away. Their voices, raucous as mad birds, carried on the sultry golden air.

Back on the main path the other kids scurried along tracks, spreading out into the bush like a network of ants.

I raced back, running until my breath burnt my chest, back to the humps of the waiting vehicles with my mother's last conversation with Lisnet echoing in my ears.

"I will love them like my own."

"Love won't fill their bellies, Martha."

"Love fills lots of gaps, my sister."

My own belly ached with emptiness and my head spun as once more I faced the man with the glittering eyes.

"There are no giraffes that way," I told him.

I've reproduced that story in order to show you that it

29

does actually work in 700 words. But could it also work as a novel? And if so, how could it be developed? Before we can find out we need to list the elements.

The Prize – the novel

The characters and premise

The main character, let's call him Samuel, has a big problem, poverty, so the stakes are certainly high enough for a novel. We know also that the boy has an aunt Lisnet who has died of the sickness (HIV). This is another big emotional issue. Samuel has a younger brother, Peter, and several cousins. His mother, Martha, is increasingly weary. Is she ill too? His father may or may not be around.

The anti-hero is the poacher who is offering him money to find a giraffe. He provides the dilemma. But in a novel perhaps he could become a viewpoint character. Why does he do it? What is his motivation? He seems unsympathetic, but could we make the reader care about him? This would be challenging and interesting.

There are a lot of characters here for a short story. They are mostly not mentioned by name – because it isn't necessary in short fiction – and it would not be necessary to develop all of them in a novel either. There would still only need to be a few main characters. Perhaps Samuel and the poacher, let's call him Jay, could be developed.

Setting

The setting is Africa, which is vibrant and visual and an interesting place to set a novel. It is also somewhere I know and care about: knowing your setting helps when

you write anything, but particularly a novel.
Metaphorically, you are going to spend a lot of time there.
It would be a shame if you hated every minute!

Conflict/theme

Poaching is at the heart of the conflict. But there are other strong themes. Survival, extinction, love.

Romance also makes a very good subplot. Perhaps Jay could have a romance with someone in the boy's family and this could complicate everything.

Or perhaps politics could become a subplot; politics and poaching would be an interesting strand to explore.

Motivation

In the short story, Samuel is idealistic. Love is more important than money. But what if this was just the beginning of the novel. What if, as a consequence of saving the giraffe, his mother died? How is this going to make him feel for the rest of his life? How will the guilt shape him and how will it determine his destiny? Perhaps he becomes a poacher himself. Or perhaps he becomes a conservationist and he and Jay are locked in conflict.

Can you see how this 700 word short story could actually quite easily become a novel if we were to explore aspects of it that there isn't room to explore in the short story? We will look at developing these aspects, that is, setting, and character in more depth in the appropriate chapters. But just for fun I've written a blurb for this 'possible novel'.

Blurb for *The Prize*

This is a story about a Kenya boy and a hunter. They first

cross swords when the boy refuses to track a rare species of giraffe. Money can't buy everything. But when his mother dies as a direct result of his refusal, his guilt haunts him. He blames the hunter and so begins a vendetta against him.

In an insane cat and mouse dance across Kenya, boy and poacher toy with each other in a series of increasingly brutal attacks. It's a battle that is complicated by love. It is a battle that neither can win. But is either of them really ready to die for their beliefs?

OK, this is pretty dire, and a lot more thought would need to go into it, but I hope you can see how it could be possible to develop a 700-word story into a novel.

I mentioned subplots. So let's have a look at them in both short and long fiction.

What is a subplot?

Subplots are used in both short and long fiction and we're going to look at examples of both. But essentially they're 'lesser' or 'supporting' plots that run alongside the main plot. They can be parallel plots that aren't strictly connected to the main plot but they touch it in places and they affect it, if only in as much as they affect the main characters. Very often they are completely entangled with it and they will enrich it in some way.

Also, a subplot will tend to reflect the main theme of the novel, hence strengthening it and adding depth.

Example of a subplot in a short story

They are not always used in short stories, they are much more often used in longer fiction, but they can work well. *Echoes in the Mineshaft* (published in *Take a Break*

Fiction Feast and also in *Fast Fiction,* Australia) was about a couple who go potholing and end up lost near an old mine shaft.

This is a dual-viewpoint time-slip story. Running alongside the main storyline is a separate story, a subplot if you like, told through the viewpoint of a child. He and his uncle were trapped in a mining accident 100 years previously. They sang songs like *Ten Green Bottles* to keep their spirits up until they were rescued. They were never rescued.

The lost couple are guided to safety to the tune of *Ten Green Bottles*. They later hear about the story of the lost miners, whose bodies were discovered years later alongside messages they scratched on the mine shaft walls to their loved ones. They also discover they are not the first lost potholers to be led to safety to the tune of *Ten Green Bottles*. The theme tying both stories together is 'lost'. In this example the main story couldn't exist without the subplot.

Example of a subplot in a novel

Subplots are more often used in novels. Let's just return briefly to my novel, *Passing Shadows*, the story of Maggie, who falls for the father of her best friend's child. (He doesn't know he's the father, a fact which brings tension and conflict.) The subplot focuses on Garry, a rather bumbling vet, and his search for love.

This subplot reflects the main theme of the novel, which is love and second chances, and in doing so it highlights and develops aspects of Maggie's character. So it's working on more than one level, which a good subplot should do.

Plotting a short story

It is perfectly possible to write a short story without having any idea of the plot before you start. Although lots of writers like to know where they're going, and this is fine too. I am not good at plotting. I much prefer to throw my characters a problem and then sit back and see how they resolve it. I know my story will emerge from this. This way of working has the advantage of making my stories character-led. At least I think it's an advantage!

I find that if I decide on the storyline first and then create characters to fit it, I often end up with characters that aren't so rounded. But this is purely personal.

Plotting a novel

It's possible to do the same with a novel, but I think it's a lot easier to know roughly where you're going – and be clear what your novel is about. You don't need to know the ins and outs of every plot twist (although some writers do). There are lots of ways to plot a novel. You can write lists from 1 to 30 of pertinent events. You can use a flowchart or a mind map. You can use Post-its with major scenes on and move them around. I don't want to get too bogged down with the nuts and bolts of writing a novel; there are dozens of books that will tell you how to do this. But what I do want to say is: think development.

Think about developing the strands that you do actually have. For example, instead of having Maggie in *Passing Shadows* rushing to deal with kidnappers and adoption and irate farmers, I realised I needed to deepen the themes that I already had in the novel, which were Maggie's deeply held beliefs that she was second best and unloved. These themes were also reflected in the animal sanctuary setting via the animals she rescued, and the other characters, who had all been let down in some way. Could there be a second chance at love for any of them?

Summary of differences

Short story plots look at one aspect of a character's life and how he reacts to it.

Novel plots look at the character's reactions in detail. How does he react to his problems and how does he deal with them and how does this change him as a person as he moves through the novel.

In a short story the character should change by the end.

In a novel he can change several times in response to how the plot progresses. Some of his changes may well seem contradictory.

Short story plots focus on the now, although they might use flashback to illustrate how a character arrived in the now.

Novel plots will almost certainly have to revisit the past in detail, via either flashback or time jumps in order to show character motivation and progression.

Chapter Five
Creating Great Characters

What is the main difference between characters in a short story and characters in a novel?

In a nutshell, the answer is, again, development. But it's not quite as simple as that. Characters in a short story can be just as well developed as characters in a novel. And by developed I mean that they will leap off the page, they will appear to be alive. They will be fully rounded individuals that the reader will care about.

I noticed, or rather my agent noticed, that when I first started writing novels my minor characters were often better developed than my main characters. This was not quite the effect I was looking for. But I think this came about because I was so accustomed to bringing characters to life with very few words, that it was easy to replicate this in my novels.

What did I do with all the extra words I had to bring my main characters to life? Well, if you've read the previous chapter you'll know that I used them to invent increasingly bizarre plot twists. I certainly didn't "waste" them on characterisation. As a result, my main characters were often a bit flat – a bit thin, and no one cared about them much, least of all me.

So my novels didn't work. This was very disappointing because I had always thought I was quite strong on characterisation. My plots were weak, I thought, so I'd been concentrating on those. And in doing so – and mucking those up too – I'd forgotten about characterisation. Never take your eye off the ball! Once again, I'd assumed that the techniques used for short stories and novels were the same.

Again, my experience tells me that I'm not the only erstwhile short-story writer who has this problem. It's often easier to make your subsidiary characters spring to life because, ironically, you don't have much time to paint them.

Here's an example of a snapshot of a minor character in *Passing Shadows*:

He'd probably drunk real ale – Tanglefoot or Pilgrim's Pride – standing with his back to the open fire, with a little frill of froth on his moustache. She was sure he'd have had a moustache, a black curly one like Agatha Christie's Poirot.

That's quite a visual description of a character, isn't it? The reader isn't likely to forget it, which would be great if they needed to remember it. But actually they don't. This character is actually dead and buried. This 'imaginary' description of him is actually only in Maggie's head and he is never mentioned again. He hardly even really qualifies as a minor character.

Another reason I think it's easy to bring minor characters to life is because you can use short story techniques, such as using a snapshot image like the one above. But while these can be effective, you'll need to do more than this to bring your main characters alive.

Introducing a character in a short story

This is an extract from a story called, *A Day in the Life of Dora Carter – aged 82 exactly* (published in *Woman's Weekly*)

Anyway, I'm there, finally. Ready to go out. I study my reflection in the wardrobe mirror. White hair neatly tucked beneath a yellow straw sun hat, which I bought in a sale because of its rather fetching pink ribbons. That's my concession to summer. I'm wearing my favourite tweed skirt and jacket too. I feel the cold a lot more than I used to. And on top of that, the emerald coat Martin got me one Christmas and a peacock blue scarf that I'm rather fond of. Oh, and a pair of socks over my woollen tights. One red sock and one canary yellow. I smile, pleased with the overall effect and grab my bag from the dressing table. Second thoughts, I won't take my bag, I don't want to encourage muggers and a white plastic bin liner will do just as well to carry my purse in.

You might possibly use this style of introduction in a novel, if it was relevant, although using a mirror to describe a character is quite a cliché. So you probably wouldn't. What I hope you're getting though, is that Dora is pretty eccentric – or at least this is the effect she wants to create. And this is what this story is all about.

Introducing a character in a novel

This is an extract from my novel, *Helter Skelter*, and introduces the hero.

According to tradition, good legs meant quality – both in

women and in horses. Garrin had always thought there were other parts of their anatomies that were equally good yardsticks. The bay horse trotting away from him had strong well-muscled hindquarters. The sort that had a nice solid feel if you slapped them. Not too much bounce, but not so firm you'd hurt your hand. If he had to score them on slapability they'd come out somewhere around factor nine, ten, being high.

The girl riding the horse didn't have a bad butt either, and, tightly encased in fawn jodhpurs as it was right now, he was in a good position to judge. She wasn't so skinny that there was no movement when she hit the saddle on the downward stride of the rising trot, but there wasn't enough of a wobble to be distracting. Women with wobbly bums were very distracting and could sometimes put him right off his stroke when he was teaching.

"Change the rein," he shouted now, because it meant she'd have to come past him again and he could have another close-up look. Yes, it really was very nice, he decided as Nero went by, his hooves thudding on the hard packed peat of the school. Pity her riding skills didn't match up. "You're too stiff," he yelled. "Loosen up a bit for Christ's sake. It's a horse, not a seesaw."

She was pretty, but she wasn't very fit. Her face was flushed and a strand of blonde hair that had escaped from her skullcap was sticking to her forehead. They were only ten minutes into the lesson. God knows what she'd be like when they really got going.

"And – walk," he ordered. "No, not like that. You're too heavy handed. You should be stopping him with your seat, not your hands. There's a mouth on the end of those reins." She didn't say anything. She looked as though she was going to burst into tears. He sighed. "Rein in."

She brought the horse to an untidy halt and he strolled

across. "Your stirrups are too long, that's not helping."
He adjusted them. "Here. That's more like it." He stood
back, a slight frown on his face. "Overall, you haven't got
a bad seat. You're too far back though; we're aiming for
a nice light, forward seat. Like this. Better. Now try
again. And for Christ's sake, look where you're going.
How's he supposed to know what you want him to do
when you've got your chin stuck in your chest?"

Strictly speaking we're introducing two characters, but as
both of them are main characters, this is fine. As you can
see, this is quite a different type of introduction. Here the
focus is on showing the character's personality, via what
he is doing.

If this was a short story I might have said, *Garrin was
a riding instructor who regularly reduced his pupils to
tears,* and then got on with the rest of the story. But this is
a novel. Horses are a big part of the plot in *Helter Skelter.*
They are a major part of Garrin's character, his
profession, in fact. So it makes sense spending some time
showing Garrin at work.

His physical appearance can come later. It's what he's
like as a person that counts. And he's not very nice – at
least not to people! He's brusque, bossy and possibly a
mite sexist, and he'd need to be a very good teacher to get
away with it, as presumably his pupil is paying him for
the lesson. As it's a novel there is plenty of time for
Garrin to redeem himself. There is plenty of time for the
reader to find out why he is so brutal to Amanda too.

This is another aspect that's different. You can take a
few more risks with characters in a novel, they can be
bigger, bolder, nastier, even when they are basically
sympathetic characters. There is time to show their back
story, their motivations in more depth.

This can come under the banner of pace. In short stories characters need to be introduced quickly, and often with some impact. In novels you have more time to bring them in.

Physical description in short stories and novels – what's the difference?

Is there a difference? Not all short story writers provide physical descriptions of their characters. But then neither do all novelists. But if you are going to provide descriptions then I think there's a difference in technique.

Using physical description in a short story

As I've said, it's probably only necessary to use physical descriptions if they strictly relevant. For example, *Seeing Red* (published in *Take a Break*) is a short story set in a hairdressing salon.

"You're really lucky having hair this thick." I hold out a section of her chestnut hair, before I start to cut it. "A lot of my ladies would kill for hair like this. And the colour's gorgeous. Do you ever henna it at all?"

"No. It's been that colour since the day I was born, so I'm told. Loads of people say I'm lucky, but actually it's a curse. It grows like wildfire. To tell you the truth, I'd love to be blonde like you, Rachel, but bleach would probably turn it green. And I got enough stick about traffic lights when I was at school."

This chunk of description is strictly relevant to the story. Otherwise it wouldn't be there. The reader isn't likely to forget it – the story is only 1000 words. Appearance won't be mentioned again until the conclusion, when readers will understand the relevance of the red hair.

Using physical description in a novel

The techniques are slightly different in a novel. I've often read extracts of unpublished novels and I've wondered what the characters look like. When I've asked the authors they've often said something like "Well, there's a description of them both on page 3."

Having a description of your characters early on in your novel is fine, but don't expect your readers to remember it if it's never reinforced. This doesn't mean you need to regularly insert the same description of your characters into the text. For example, you don't need to remind us your main character wears glasses and has a slender figure every time we meet her, but you do need to find more oblique ways of reminding us until the picture is firmly established.

Perhaps you could have her forgetting her glasses and not being able to see a menu. Or perhaps you could get across her slender figure by having her buying a size ten outfit in a shop (lucky lady) or even by describing the way she moves. She flitted, as opposed to, she lumbered.

In a short story we can look back if we need to clarify what a character looks like. In a novel we don't want to have to look back thirty pages to see if the heroine had brown eyes or blue.

Parents, friends and history

When you're writing a short story your main character doesn't need parents and friends and history and a job, well not unless they are strictly relevant to the plot. She can just appear fully formed and all of these things can be hinted at or not mentioned at all. The reader will assume she has them.

In a novel, your main characters are going to need parents, friends, a job, a history. They will not be rounded people without them. This can make life slightly more complicated. After all, your character's job might not be relevant to the story. You may not want to have scenes unfolding at her workplace. If you don't, then you are going to need to find a good reason to skip them. Likewise, if you don't want her parents around, they will need to be dispensed with.

She will need a history though, and friends, and exes if she is of a certain age, and you will need to have thought through things like where she was brought up and who the important influences are in her life and what kind of education she has had, even if these are never mentioned in the novel. She must be a product of her environment if she is to be believable.

It's helpful to know these things, just as it's helpful to know her date of birth and what star sign she is – is she the type of person who checks her horoscope or mocks them?

I found when I started writing novels that this history was one of the biggest differences when it came to developing characters. I had to know much more about the characters that populated my novels than I had ever needed to know about the ones who starred in my short stories.

One viewpoint or several? – short stories

Whether you should have one viewpoint or several is a

relatively easy question to answer when it comes to short story writing. Almost always in a short story you would stick to one viewpoint. You don't have to stick to one, of course, but often your story will be stronger if you do. My first writing tutor, Jean Dynes, was very strict on viewpoint. Stick to one viewpoint or you'll confuse the reader. My next writing tutor, Ian Burton, had similar views. Go out of viewpoint at your peril. So perhaps I'm a little prejudiced, but my experience has taught me that they're right. Most short stories that flit in and out of viewpoint or are told with an omnipresent viewpoint are at worst confusing and at best weaker than single viewpoint stories.

This doesn't mean it never works. I've read some fine dual viewpoint stories or stories where the twist relies on a viewpoint change, and actually I think this is the key. Only use more than one viewpoint in a short story if you have a very good reason, and if you understand what you're doing.

One viewpoint or several? – novels

Novel writing is different. You have the freedom to use more than one viewpoint. Again, you don't have to, you can stick to one character's view of events if you prefer, but I think that having more than one viewpoint in a novel can actually have the opposite effect to having more than one in a short story. It can strengthen your narrative. And I think this is because seeing things through more than one character's eyes can add depth and understanding.

Before you go charging off rubbing your hands in glee with a plan to have half a dozen viewpoints in your novel, I'd like to add a note of caution. The writer should always be in control of viewpoint. Characters should only have a viewpoint if it's essential to the story and by that I mean it should move the plot or characters forward in some way, it should give information that the reader has no other way of knowing.

Having too many viewpoints in a novel is just as confusing as having too many in a short story. A writer has to be quite skilful to handle a lot – or to use an omnipresent viewpoint without losing their readers.

Have I chosen the right viewpoint character?

Again, this is a relatively easy question to answer with a short story. I think when you've written a few it's instinctive anyway. But if it's not, just ask yourself whose story it is. The chances are the answer will determine your viewpoint character.

I think this can also work well in a novel. Whose story is it? But maybe it's more than one person's story. Let's go back to my hypothetical novel, *The Prize*. Is it Samuel's story, or is it Jay's, the poacher's? This story could be told via just one of their viewpoints, but I think it's probably better told via two viewpoints (or perhaps even three if we have a subplot like romance, for example). Then we can understand all the characters' motivations and perspectives.

This is often the case with longer pieces of work. Although I do still think there should be a primary main character. In this case my instinct tells me it should be Samuel, as he is likely to be most sympathetic of the two. The primary main character should have more of the viewpoint than any other viewpoint character and very often, although not always, the novel will begin in their viewpoint too.

Which characters have which scenes?

Another question to ask if you're going to have more than one viewpoint character is how you decide whose viewpoint to use in each scene. Again, this is often instinctive but if it isn't, a good rule of thumb is to look at the emotional stakes. Which of your characters cares the most? For example, if you're writing a scene in which a child has gone missing, then think about who will care the most. Chances are it will be the mother or father, but this will depend on the story. Perhaps the parents don't care about the child and it's her sister who cares the most, or her grandmother. Whoever cares the most should probably be the viewpoint character.

Incidentally, it's generally better, particularly if you are starting off as a novel writer, not to change viewpoint too frequently at first. Establish your viewpoint character firmly, before taking the reader out of his or her head and into someone else's. If you change viewpoint too often you run the risk of the reader losing interest.

I will go into viewpoint in more depth in the next chapter.

Summary of differences

Short story characters can be introduced quickly and with a bang, if necessary.

Novel characters can be built up in a more leisurely way.

Physical characteristics of your short story characters can be introduced straight away, or left out altogether. In a novel, the way your characters look will need to be reinforced subtly and quite often if it's important that the reader knows what they look like.

Short stories tend to have a single viewpoint.

There is much more flexibility in a novel. Decide which character has the viewpoint in either form by establishing which character cares the most.

Short story characters don't need relations, best friends and histories.

Novel characters must have relations, best friends and histories.

Chapter Six
Viewpoint and Tense

We touched on viewpoint in the last chapter but I'd like to go into it in a bit more detail as it still raises lots of questions with writers, both when it comes to short stories and novels.

Single viewpoint short stories

Short stories where one character has all the viewpoint are probably the easiest to write. The viewpoint character is usually the main character too, so everything is nice and neat. There isn't much room for confusion and it's relatively easy to stay in one viewpoint for the duration of one or two thousand words.

Single viewpoint stories can be written in first or third person and either in past or present tense. You can, if you wish, vary the tenses, so, for example, you start in present tense and flick into the past tense, but if you do this, make sure you have a good reason. I'm not so keen on switching between first and third person in short stories as it can be a bit cumbersome. But I have seen it done successfully in more literary fiction.

Single viewpoint novels

It's perhaps slightly harder to write a single viewpoint

novel for the simple reason that it's a lot longer to be confined to one viewpoint. Your story can only unfold through the eyes of one character. You can't, for example, leave one character in a cliffhanger situation, while you switch into another character's viewpoint. See example below:

Sarah knew she shouldn't have come into the empty house when she heard the tread of heavy footsteps on the stairs. Panicking, she ran up to the attic. For a few moments the footsteps hesitated and then, slowly but surely, she heard them coming up the final flight...

Dennis knew Sarah was in danger, they'd always had the same telepathy, and right at this moment she was in serious trouble. He could feel it. Without stopping to question his instincts, he flicked his car keys off the hook.

Heart thumping, he ran through the rain to his car, jumped in, started the ignition and pulled away. It was only as he reached the bottom of the drive that he realised something was wrong with his car. The steering was odd. Cursing he slewed to a halt and pulled his coat up around his ears as he got out to check. What a time to get a flat.

Now, if this was a single viewpoint novel we wouldn't be able to leave Sarah in danger of 'heaven knows what' while we flicked across to see what Dennis was up to. We would have to stay with her while the heavy footsteps approached. As the author you would have to find another way of increasing tension – perhaps she could jump into a cupboard and the footsteps could come right into the room but not find her. Perhaps another character could turn up.

Naturally, even if you did use Dennis's viewpoint as

well, then sooner or later you would have to take the reader back to Sarah, but it's possible, for example, that Dennis could arrive too late and find Sarah kidnapped or even dead, depending on which way you wanted your plot to go.

You couldn't do this if the viewpoint was Sarah's alone. Well, I guess there's always the possibility of having the rest of her story told from some unearthly plane, that's been done a few times lately. But if you were writing a straight thriller this might be tricky. So, with a multi viewpoint novel there are more choices. A single viewpoint novel has limitations.

No viewpoint or several in a short story

Of course you don't have to use viewpoint at all in a short story. It's possible to have a short story unfold via dialogue and action and never introduce the reader to anyone's thoughts or feelings.

It's also possible to tell the reader how *every* character in the story feels and what they are thinking – this is sometimes called head hopping. This can work, but in my experience it requires a great deal of skill to pull it off. There is a big danger that without a viewpoint at all (or with several viewpoints) the reader won't know a) whose story it is or b) who to care about, so they will end up not caring at all. This can sometimes work if the plot is strong enough to carry it. But it is a risk.

Using a narrator in a short story

I think it's slightly easier to use a narrator in a short story because at least the narrator has a distinctive voice. But if you do use a narrator be careful that you don't distance the reader too much from the characters.

Incidentally, just to clarify, when I say using a narrator I mean using a narrator who is not also a character.

Here's an example of a narrator's voice in a short story:

This is the story of how my father met my mother. It was a winter's night in 1966 and had been snowing heavily. My father was very tired and on his way back from a meeting, my mother had been walking home from a party when she slipped on some ice and broke her leg.

Unless you have a good reason for using a narrator, for example, these past events have a strong bearing on what is happening now, why not simply use the mother or father's viewpoint without adding the extra distance of a narrator. Do not just use a narrator for the sake of it.

No viewpoint or several in a novel

I think it would be quite hard to write a novel with no viewpoint at all, although I stand to be corrected on that one. However, lots of novels are written with several viewpoints. We touched on this in the previous chapter. So I'm not going to repeat myself, but generally the rule would be: less is more.

Using a narrator in a novel

The writers of the past, Dickens for example, often used a separate narrator to tell the story. This narrator would be aware of what was happening in every character's life. This is similar to using an omnipresent viewpoint where the author lets the reader know what is happening in every person's life, but in the latter there is no separate narrator.

It is not so common to use a separate narrator today, although anything is possible. If you really want to try this approach then why not?

However, it's more usual to write a novel using one of the characters as the narrator, that is, your viewpoint character becomes your narrator.

Unreliable narrators

These can be used in short stories or longer fiction and they simply mean that the narrator can't be taken at face value.

In the short story, a monologue can be a very effective way of using a narrator who is not quite reliable. For example, our main character, Sue, might be ranting and raving about her terrible neighbours who are always complaining unnecessarily and who make her life hell. Only for us to later discover, through what Sue is telling us, that actually it's Sue who is the terrible neighbour. It's actually Sue who is deluded, although obviously she won't know that herself, which is why the reader doesn't know it straight away. Although at first we empathise with Sue, as the story unfolds we slowly switch our allegiance to her 'poor' neighbours who are the real victims.

Unreliable narrators can be used to very good effect in a novel. Perhaps the main character is deluded or insane. Perhaps he is a drug addict or an alcoholic in denial. Marion Keyes did this very well in her novel, *Rachel's Holiday*. At first it seems possible that Rachel is actually just a good-time girl, who goes slightly over the top with recreational drugs sometimes. But as the novel progresses we, the readers, realise that she's actually in complete denial about her drug addiction. Of course, we cannot discover this totally until Rachel herself realises. Although we might suspect the truth before this point.

Although unreliable narrators are most often used in first-person novels, there's no reason why you shouldn't use the techniques in other types of novel. Don't forget though, that for this to work your characters must believe they are telling the truth. You can't just have them lying unconvincingly to themselves for the purpose of your plot. If you do, the reader will be left feeling cheated.

Advantages of first and third person in the short story

It used to be said that using first person in a story made readers feel closer to the character, that is, they were taken right inside the character's head. Also, everything the character experienced would be seen through his or her eyes so every description or feeling would be flavoured with that character's voice.

But I'm not so sure this is the case these days. You can take the reader just as close to the character in third person, as long as you adhere to the same rules, that is, you make sure that all descriptions and feelings are in the character's own voice and not the author's.

Perhaps it's easier to stay inside a character's head in first person. Here's an example.

I moved a little closer to the monkey's cage. Then I checked over my shoulder. Mum was too busy talking to Kate to notice what I was doing. I got out the banana and shoved it through the bars. I thought maybe I should have peeled it, but the monkey didn't care. He grabbed at it, and for a second our fingers touched. His were hairy, but pink underneath...

It is easy in first person to stay inside the child's viewpoint. In third person it's more tempting to come outside it.

Six-year-old Jack moved a little closer to the macaque's enclosure. He checked over his shoulder but his mother was oblivious to what he was doing. She was talking to his auntie Kate. He rummaged in his bag for the banana she'd given him for his lunch. Then he slipped it through the bars of the cage to the waiting macaque.

There is nothing (superficially) wrong with this third person version, apart from, possibly, he wouldn't refer to himself as six-year-old Jack. But there might be a lot wrong depending on the character. Does Jack know, for example, that the monkey is a macaque and would he call the cage an enclosure? Would he say Auntie Kate? This informs the reader, but is it his viewpoint? Would he use words like 'rummaged' and 'slipped'? Would he say, 'the banana she'd given him for his lunch.' (He knows she gave him the banana for lunch – he doesn't need to inform the reader.)

He might well do and say all of these things. He might be an expert on different types of monkey, or he might have read the sign – is there a sign? But I hope you can see what I'm getting at. If you are truly in your character's viewpoint you can only use language he will know. You cannot be in a child's viewpoint, either in first person or third person, and have him use words he would not know. Not even in narrative.

At the risk of boring you to tears, here's the passage one

54

more time. This time in third person again, but strictly in Jack's viewpoint.

He moved a bit closer to the monkey's cage. Then he checked over his shoulder. Mum was too busy talking to see what he was up to. He got out the banana and pushed it through the bars. Maybe he should have peeled it, but the monkey didn't care. The monkey whizzed down and grabbed it. It was a shock when their fingers touched, but really cool too. He sniffed his fingers to see if the monkey's scent was on his hand, but he could just smell banana. Hey, just wait till he told Ella.

This last passage is still in third person, but it does not stray out of Jack's viewpoint, either in experience levels or vocabulary. I hope it captures a little of his voice – the more you can do that in your writing the better your characterisation will be.

So I truly don't think it matters these days if you want to use first person or third for your short story. You can get just as close to the character in either type of viewpoint. You can use internal monologues equally well in first or third person, these days.

Advantages of first and third person in the novel

I think that all of the above also applies to novels. And I think we have covered whether to use one viewpoint or multiple with Sarah and Dennis. But what if you want to use both first and third person in a novel?

Some authors use this as a device. For example, they might tell their novel from two or more viewpoints in sections, having each section headed up with the name of the viewpoint character (this works in longer short stories too).

They might also differentiate whose viewpoint it is by having one character in third person and one character in first person. With care, they'll differentiate their viewpoint in other ways too. Their characters' voices should, as we've said, be quite different and distinctive.

There's no reason why you shouldn't do this in a novel. But equally I think there ought to be a good reason for doing it. By all means experiment, but if you find that your writing starts to seem pretentious or you are thinking more about the technical side than the characters or plot, you might want to reconsider. Why complicate things unnecessarily?

One more thing to add: it's worth bearing in mind that some publishers of short stories prefer third person and some prefer first. And this applies to novels too. If you are writing to sell, then check the publisher's preferences.

Should I use present tense or past?

Using present tense for short stories is perfectly acceptable. It will suit some short story plots better than past tense, particularly if they are also written in first person. Let your instincts guide you.

Using present tense in novels is, I feel, slightly more of a challenge. Some readers (and some publishers) absolutely hate it. It can be exhausting to read and it can also feel contrived. It's not too much of a problem to use present tense for the whole of a short story because it's such a short time span, but to keep it going for a whole novel is trickier.

Having said that, if it is done incredibly skilfully, think Sophie Kinsella, it can work fine. The reader may not even notice. Once again, though, I think present tense works better in first person, than it does in third. But maybe this is personal preference.

Example one – first person, present tense

The drive over is tense, but I don't realise how terrified I am until I'm actually standing outside no 5. The building doesn't help; dark and unwelcoming, with steep steps and no handrail. I'd hate to tackle them in icy weather. Maybe Stephen does it on purpose, I think. Maybe he just doesn't like visitors. It wouldn't surprise me. He was always a loner. He can't have changed that much since we were children.

I go up cautiously and ring the bell. I can hear it echoing distantly.

Someone in a butler's outfit answers the door. He doesn't smile. I've half a mind to run away.

Example two – third person, present tense

The drive over is tense, but Karen doesn't realise how terrified she is until she is actually standing outside no 5. The building doesn't help; It's dark and unwelcoming, with steep steps and no handrail. She'd hate to tackle them in icy weather. Maybe Stephen does it on purpose, she thinks. Maybe he just doesn't like visitors. It wouldn't surprise her. He was always a loner. He can't have changed that much since they were children.

She goes up cautiously and rings the bell. She can hear it echoing distantly. Someone in a butler's outfit answers the door. He doesn't smile. She's got half a mind to run away.

I think that third person present tense is fine for a while, but it can get cumbersome as the characters move around the novel. If you have to say, he *does* this, or he *says* this constantly it can become quite hard work for the reader. But as I say this is just my opinion. Maybe you feel the same way about first person present tense.

Write in whatever tense feels comfortable and right for your novel.

Summary of differences

Single viewpoint short stories are probably the easiest form to get right, both in terms of character and plot.

Single viewpoint novels can be *more* restricting and actually *harder* to plot than multi viewpoint novels.

Using multi viewpoint in a short story can be confusing.

Using multi viewpoint in a novel can add depth.

First person present tense short stories work well.

First person present tense novels are much harder to sustain.

Using a narrator or omnipresent viewpoint can work in either form but in a short story you are likely to distance the reader from the characters using this viewpoint.

Unreliable narrators work equally well in both forms.

Chapter Seven
Dialogue

How does dialogue in a novel differ from that in a short story?

Well, to give a very tongue-in-cheek answer, the main difference is there's a lot more of it. So it's important that you get your characters' voices right.

Just to illustrate what I'm talking about, let's look at an average short story, of about one thousand words. I think it's fair to say that you'd have about thirty or forty per cent dialogue, which equates to about three or four hundred words. You'll obviously have more than one voice in there (otherwise it wouldn't be dialogue) but the reader isn't going to notice too much if your characters sound alike, simply because there isn't enough dialogue to make it that obvious.

In a novel it is completely different. Using the same principle, in a ninety thousand word novel you're going to have about thirty thousand words of dialogue. Are your readers going to notice if all your characters speak with the same voice? Yes, they most certainly are.

Does it matter if all my characters speak with the same voice?

Well, while you might get away with it in a short story,

although personally I think it's better to give characters individual voices, if you do this in a novel there's a danger that your characters will become cardboard cut-outs whose sole purpose is to carry the plot.

If the plot's really gripping, will the readers care? Well, maybe they won't care, but if you want to write a good novel *you* should care. Good writing is about good characterisation and dialogue is a massive part of characterisation.

How do I stop them all sounding like me?

When I write dialogue, like lots of writers, I don't feel as if I'm really writing it, more as though I'm transcribing it. One of my characters will begin a conversation and another one will answer and I just write it down. I don't sit and think about what they might say, it just comes naturally.

It's interesting, but until I just wrote that last paragraph I had no idea that's what I did. I'm not an audio writer. I don't actually 'hear' characters voices in my head – at least not very often, but I do know what they're going to say. And this only happens when I know them well. Just as in real life if you know a person well, you often know what she's going to say in a given situation. This, for me, is the essence of writing good dialogue. Make your characters truly alive and then sit back and transcribe what they say.

How do I handle dialect and rhythms of speech?

My feelings about reproducing dialect on the page are very simple. Less is more. And that applies to both short stories and novels, particularly when it comes to phonetically spelled words. I don't know about you but I find there is nothing more off-putting than picking up a short story or novel and being faced with a big section of phonetically spelled words that are hard to read and even harder to interpret.

For the last two years I've been an editor for a publisher so I read for a living as well as for pleasure and when it comes to the pleasure side of it, I don't want to struggle too much. I don't want to wade through streams of phonetic spelling. I don't want to have to try and decipher what the characters are saying. If it's too annoying I stop reading. Maybe this is lazy. Maybe I should persevere, but this is how I feel. And I've spoken to a lot of people who feel the same. I want the writer to struggle – so I don't have to!

On the other hand, there is certainly a place for dialect. Written sensitively and used sparingly it can enhance characterisation like nothing else. I particularly like the way Kathryn Stockett used it in her novel *The Help*. She also used rhythms of speech very well and this novel is worth checking out just as an illustration of how to write excellent dialogue. It's an excellent read as well!

Just one more point on rhythms of language; you'd be surprised how much we absorb on a subconscious level. Consider, for example, how much easier it is to learn a language when you are actually in the country of origin. We seem to absorb rhythms of language almost through our skin. So if you want to write great Scottish dialogue, my best advice is to go to Scotland or find some Scottish friends to listen to.

If you use a sprinkling of dialect and you also make full use of rhythms of speech your characters will come alive, regardless of whether you write short stories or novels. However, in my experience, readers are often prepared to work harder when reading a novel than a short story.

Characterisation through dialogue

As I've already mentioned, dialogue is a massive part of characterisation, although it's not just how characters say things, it's what they say. Let your characters show their true natures through everything they say, or don't say. Are they kind, cruel, mean, posh, uneducated, pompous, controlling, egocentric, selfish, gossipy? The list is pretty much endless. Every time your characters open their mouths they should reveal something about themselves. But if you know who they are, then chances are this will happen naturally.

How do I check my dialogue is working?

In real life dialogue is spoken aloud, so a good way to test it in fiction is to read it out. Interestingly though, dialogue that is written for the stage, that is for actors' mouths, and dialogue that is part of a novel are not quite the same thing.

For the stage dialogue must stand alone, but if it's part of a short story or novel it doesn't have to stand alone. It is being supported by the surrounding narrative. This might sound strange but it's true. Look at the following piece of dialogue, which is an extract from *Passing Shadows*. All the narrative has been removed. All that is left is direct dialogue.

"Are you too tired to walk back? I could call us a taxi."

"No, let's walk. I'm just getting my second wind. What's the night life like here?"

"You never stop surprising me. I haven't a clue. But if you're not tired I could give you the grand tour. Dad brought me here quite a bit when I was a kid. It was the closest beach."

"Will we be able to get back into the hotel?"

"I've got a front door key. It's not like the old days of seaside landladies, you know. They don't lock you out if you're not back by eleven."

"Lead on, McTaggart."

"We used to come for the day quite often, and a day was a whole day. No messing about. We'd catch the train, get here about eight and then walk around shivering in our shorts and T-shirts until the sun warmed us up. Dad always insisted we wore our shorts because we were at the beach and it was bound to be sunny."

"And was it? I thought Skegness had a reputation for bracing winds."

"It does, but whatever the weather we had a strict routine. Breakfast in a beach café, slot machines until lunch time and then the theme park. That was always Dad's favourite."

"He liked going on rides?"

"Oh, he didn't go on anything. He liked watching me clinging on for dear life. He used to stand on the ground slapping his leg every time my carriage came past and roaring with laughter. I bet he didn't strike you as sadistic, did he? I was terrified most of the time."

"You weren't, were you? I can't imagine you being terrified of anything."

"You'd be surprised. I'm winding you up, Maggie. It was a good sort of terror. The sort that gets your heart thumping, even though you know you're quite safe, really."

Does it feel a little bit flat to you? A little bit lifeless. It should do because it was never meant to stand alone.

Saying that, I deliberately picked a section of dialogue which doesn't have much supporting narrative, but what was there was necessary.

Here it is with the narrative put back in.

"Are you too tired to walk back?" Finn asked, when they finally rolled out of the door at half past eleven. "I could call us a taxi."

"No, let's walk. I'm just getting my second wind. What's the night life like here?"

"You never stop surprising me." He shook his head. "I haven't a clue. But if you're not tired I could give you the grand tour. Dad brought me here quite a bit when I was a kid. It was the closest beach."

"Will we be able to get back into the hotel?"

"I've got a front door key. It's not like the old days of seaside landladies, you know. They don't lock you out if you're not back by eleven."

She smiled. "Lead on, McTaggart."

They went past a theme park and he pointed out the big wheel and the roller coaster, which were shadowed and silent, like great, hulking monsters, asleep until daylight.

"We used to come for the day quite often," Finn said. "And a day was a whole day. No messing about. We'd catch the train, get here about eight and then walk around shivering in our shorts and T-shirts until the sun warmed us up. Dad always insisted that we wore our shorts because we were at the beach and it was bound to be sunny."

"And was it?" Maggie asked, fascinated. "I thought Skegness had a reputation for bracing winds."

"It does, but whatever the weather we had a strict routine. Breakfast in a beach café, slot machines until lunch time and then the theme park. That was always Dad's favourite."

"He liked going on rides?"

"Oh, he didn't go on anything. He liked watching me clinging on for dear life. He used to stand on the ground slapping his leg every time my carriage came past and roaring with laughter. I bet he didn't strike you as sadistic, did he? I was terrified most of the time."

"You weren't, were you? I can't imagine you being terrified of anything."

"You'd be surprised." His face darkened and then he grinned. "I'm winding you up, Maggie. It was a good sort of terror. The sort that gets your heart thumping, even though you know you're quite safe, really."

She nodded, aware that her own heart was thumping a bit. She couldn't decide whether it was his proximity, or simply because they were in an unfamiliar town at night.

I hope you can see that the second version is more complete, more rounded. The narrative is also used to balance sentences. Although speech tags are not needed necessarily to inform the reader who is talking, they are often used purely for balance, or to show hesitation.

For example, "We used to come for the day quite often," Finn said. "And a day was a whole day. No messing about."

We don't need the words, 'Finn said', we know who is talking from the context, but they do balance the sentence. And they also give a pause. So it reads as though he has paused slightly between sentences, even though I haven't actually written, 'he paused'.

It's worth being aware of how speech verbs can be

used like this. Sometimes they can be used in place of en dashes or other punctuation, sometimes they can be used in place of accompanying phrases, for example, he paused.

Try removing the narrative from sections of your own dialogue. It's a fascinating exercise. And if the dialogue that remains falls slightly flat, you're probably getting the balance about right.

How do I check my narrative is working?

In this chapter I've talked a lot about dialogue, but writing is all about balance. By balance I'm really talking abut the lengths of words and sentences you're using and how they fit together as a whole. It's possible, for example, to fall into the trap of having sentences that are all the same length, whether that's short or long, but pace means that you need a variety.

Balance is one of the things you can work on when you edit your drafts. It doesn't necessarily come naturally on a first draft, although I find that the more practice I have the better I get at it. Getting the balance right is, I feel, a mixture of craft and instinct.

Once again, a good way to check that what you're writing has good balance is to read it aloud. This is also a good way to check punctuation. If you're gasping for breath, then your sentences are probably too long. This could also happen if they're too short, and the pace is too fast.

I have a personal theory – and this probably sounds mad – but it works for me: if you read something aloud and it has perfect balance you can *dance* to the narrative. It will have its own rhythm and you can literally move your body in time to the rhythm. This only works if you read a manuscript aloud.

Try it for yourself and you'll see what I mean.

Summary of differences

If you're writing a short story readers may not notice if the characters' voices are not distinctive and unique.

In a novel they almost certainly will. The hallmark of good characters is to recognise their voices without needing the accompanying speech tags.

Dialect and phonetic spelling can turn readers off, but they may well be more forgiving if it is in a novel than if it is in a short story. Readers often expect to work harder at a novel than a short story.

Use rhythms of speech to distinguish your characters' voices especially in a novel.

Chapter Eight
Showing and Telling

What's the difference?

I have decided to devote a whole, if short, chapter to this subject because it causes so much confusion amongst writers. What exactly does it mean, and is there a difference between showing and telling when it comes to writing short stories and writing novels?

In my view it's not so much that there's a difference, showing and telling are the same in both forms. However, you will have to do far more showing in a novel than you ever could or would need to in a short story.

In a short story you can, if you wish, get away with a great deal of telling. I would also like to add here that telling is not necessarily wrong or inferior to showing, both are necessary in fiction, but once again this will come down to balance. You will need to show, or, to put it another way, write scenically in a novel.

How do you write scenically?

The easiest way to begin to do this is to imagine that what you are writing is going to be shown on television. Think visually. To demonstrate exactly what I am talking about I have reproduced part of a short story which begins with a chunk of telling.

Telling – an example

The Weight of a Soul (published in *Woman's Weekly*)

They said she was an earth mother, which made Ellen laugh because she was neither of these things – she was an air creature with winged feet, or at least a winged imagination – and she was not a mother.

Although not for want of trying, she thought without the spike of pain that once that acknowledgment would have brought. She and Jack had tried many times to be parents: from the sighs of satisfaction after a 'hard day's work' coupling – to the 'glimpses of ecstasy' coupling after they'd been to the theatre and watched someone else's fairy tale. It was odd how theatre did that to you. It swept you up in its glitter and its romance and it made you become someone else. Just for a brief while.

This opening would be very difficult to reproduce on television. There is no setting for a start. There is no dialogue either. It is in Ellen's viewpoint, but it is mostly introspection and back story which is told directly to the reader. We know Ellen's problem is infertility – that is all. The story carries on in this vein as we learn a bit more about the couple, but we are still being told the information.

Jack had never been a great fan of the theatre but he went because she liked it. **Aspects of Love** *was her favourite musical and* **Love Changes Everything** *her favourite song. Children changed everything too, if you had them, and if you didn't it changed everything in a different way.*

However, in the section that follows, although we are still

being *told* not *shown* the information, we are getting closer to something that could be shown.

It had bothered her when she was young – their infertility. It was difficult to be a farmer's wife and be barren. Difficult to watch the lambs come each season pushed out by their mothers onto the damp earth, difficult to bottle-feed the sickly ones, cradling them by the great range oven, as they clung on to life, sucking and greedy. As the years had gone past it was difficult even to watch the new grass on the fallow fields each spring, everything reproducing, renewing itself – everything except her.

She'd felt a failure because she and Jack had never united to create another soul. Sometimes Ellen wondered if they had ever truly united. If she was a creature of the air, Jack was a creature of the land. His footfall solid as the furrows of earth he trod daily. He was a corduroy-brown man with weathered cheeks and broken veins and the scent of fresh air in his bones.

Just as an experiment I've translated some of this *told* part into a scene.

In order to show the above information a slightly different format is required. There are many ways to do this, but I've decided on two linked scenes. The first one gives us the information that Ellen can't have children of her own – by way of introducing a third character. It's mostly in dialogue. Dialogue is almost always *showing*.

Showing – an example

"Ginny, what a lovely surprise, I didn't know you were coming by."

"Max wanted to say thank you for his birthday present.

70

Say thank you, Max."

"Thank you, Auntie Ellen."

"You're very welcome sweetheart." Ellen held open the door so Ginny could manoeuvre the buggy into the hall.

"Is it OK if I leave her here for a mo where it's quiet – she'll be grumpy if I wake her?"

"Course it is – we'll hear her if she wakes up." Ellen glanced wistfully into the buggy. "We'll just be through here. Will I make tea?"

"Do I ever say no to a cuppa?" As they sipped it, sitting either end of the old oak table in the cavernous farmhouse kitchen, the conversation moved on to more specific things.

"When we spoke on the phone you said you were tired – you're not ..."

"No, I'm not pregnant, Ginny, just worn out with lambing. It's never going to happen for me and Jack. I've given up hope of it ever happening ... I'm too old now." She forced a smile. "A farmer's wife who can't breed, hey, whatever next!"

The next scene shows the damage this has caused to Jack and Ellen's marriage.

Jack hesitated in the doorway. Ellen was standing at the sink, unaware of his presence. As he watched she squirted milk onto the back of her hand, testing the temperature, which mustn't be too hot or too cold. Her shoulders were hunched, as if with grief and there was an odd stiffness about her as she moved. She was holding the bottle at arm's length as if it pained her to have it in her hands at all. Jack knew suddenly that it did. The twin lambs mewling and snuffling by the old range stove were a poor

71

substitute for a bairn of her own.

"Anything I can do?" He moved across the kitchen, his heavy boots scraping the flagstones.

"I'll thank you not to muddy my floor." Her voice was sharp, but her eyes were sad. There were deep lines around them he hadn't noticed before and shadows darkened her cheekbones. They were both getting older.

He wanted to hold her and moved as if to do so, but she brushed past him and scooped up a lamb.

"Have you finished outside, Jack?"

"Aye, I'm done for now."

"Then leave us be, there's nothing you can do here."

She picked up the lamb and turned her back on him.

This is the difference really between showing and telling. They both have a place when you're writing fiction, but if you're writing a novel, then, generally, you're going to have to do far more showing than telling. A novel by its nature moves along scenically. The human brain remembers things better when they are shown in pictures so showing is also more accessible for readers.

Showing uses far more words than telling, and it's usually, but not always, a more vivid method of writing. Don't make the mistake of thinking you have to show every little piece of information in a novel though – you don't. But showing is where the drama is to be found. If a scene is vitally important, we, the readers, should live it with the characters.

We should experience it alongside them, through their eyes and in their heads. This is the value of showing.

Incidentally, the reason I didn't use showing initially in the story, *The Weight of a Soul,* was because the story wasn't about infertility, well not directly, it was about immortality and whether having children gives you that. It was set at Jack's funeral, which was actually shown as a scene. The entire story was only 1000 words so the past couldn't have been shown, nor did it really need to be.

If ever you're in doubt about whether you should be showing a scene or simply skimming through it, then this is not a bad yardstick to use. How important is the information you need to get across? If the information is vital and integral to the plot, then it's probably better you make it into a scene and show the reader, rather than tell them what has occurred.

Conversely, if you're writing crime your clues can be hidden more effectively by telling readers about them, rather than showing them visually, and this will work even better if you do that just before a big visual scene unfolds.

Lots of information in a novel is not shown. We wouldn't see – or expect to see – every meal time and every night's sleep your character has. We would assume these had taken place. But if the story was about your character's rocky marriage, then we should certainly see a few scenes where this is evident. Showing is part of what makes us care for a character.

Summary of differences

It is necessary to *tell* the reader a fair bit of information in short stories, leaving only the important scenes to be *shown*. If you find that your short story is nearly all *told* – it's possible you are trying to cram too much into it and you should revise. Perhaps you're trying to cram a novel idea into a short story space.

When you're writing a novel, you will tend to *show* much

more. Showing the characters moving through different events is what gives a novel some of its depth. In a novel, if you ever find you are lacking depth it's often because you've done too much telling and you are not exploring scenes to their full potential.

If you do too much telling in a novel the reader will miss things. We tend to absorb information much better when we see it visually. Therefore, telling could be used as a device, for example, hiding clues in our crime novel.

I'll just duck while all those crime writers out there hit me for 'cheating the reader' with such a heinous sneaky manoeuvre.

Chapter Nine
Pace – The Beginning

For me, pace is one of the main differences between short stories and novels. The rate at which the action unfolds is vastly different in a short story to what it is in a novel – obviously it has to be. Pace was also the thing I found hardest to get right when I began to write longer fiction.

How does pace differ in short and long fiction?

A short story unfolds faster than a novel does – right? Well, yes, but it's not quite as simple as that. There are some very fast-paced novels out there and there are some very leisurely paced short stories. Once again, the easiest way to show pace is via some examples. And where better to start than the first page?

What should be on the first page of a novel?

I once did a study of first pages of novels. I wanted to know exactly what the first page of a successful novel contained. It was very interesting research and I've summarised it here.

Below is a list of the elements that appeared most often on a first page. I looked mainly at best-selling novels, so these are commercial first pages. But I think this list would apply to other types of novel too, with the possible exception of very literary fiction.

A hook

Every first page I researched had a hook. It didn't have to be dramatic, although it often was. But it did have to be there. By a hook, I mean an event that makes the reader want to read on. These are often points of change in the main character's life. They might be simple changes, for example, she is going off for an interview for a new job, or they might be big changes, she is packing a suitcase in order to leave her husband.

But there must be enough of a hook to make the reader want to turn the page and indeed get past the first paragraph. In short, there must be enough happening. Readers need to be immediately engaged, or they might not buy the book.

Short stories also need a strong hook, but in a short story, the hook could be as simple as a line of intriguing dialogue.

In both types of fiction the hook should be relevant to what is about to unfold. So you do need to think quite carefully about your hook in a novel. It would be a bit pointless to start with a dramatic event that has no further relevance to your plot.

At least one character

All the first pages I looked at introduced at least one character. This was usually the main character or someone closely connected to the main character. If it wasn't the main character there was a good reason, for example, a thriller may start with a minor character being killed. The main character will come in a little later to help track down the killer.

This works exactly the same in short stories, except in short stories it is a lot more unusual to start with a character who isn't the main character.

Setting

While the setting doesn't have to be spelt out on the first page of a novel, there isn't much room in what amounts to just under 300 words, there was usually a good indication of where the novel was taking place, for example, an urban area, or a village, which country, or even simply, the immediate surroundings, for example, the characters might be on a train or a plane and we would know roughly their location.

Short stories are the same. Setting should be there from the outset, although it is not as essential as it is in novels, and it's unnecessary to give so much detail. In fact, it's perfectly feasible to write an entire short story without ever revealing full details of where the action is taking place. As long as the reader has a rough idea, for example, a kitchen, the beach, the zoo, this is fine. You don't need to tell them the name of the town or even the name of the zoo.

In a novel you would be telling the reader these things. They expect a lot more detail. As the novel unfolds they will want to know exactly where the action is taking place, the town, be it made up or real, and the county or rough area in the country, and they will want to see the characters interacting with the setting.

A strong sense of place can add a lot of depth to a novel. In some types of novel, for example, regional sagas, it's as important as the characters.

Time

On most of the first pages I read it was immediately clear whether the novel was historical or contemporary or set in the future? It was common, when the novel wasn't contemporary, for the date to be marked above the text.

This applies to short stories too. It's perfectly acceptable to use a date, although, interestingly, because short stories tend to be set over shorter time spans than novels they are far more likely to be headed up with, for example, days of the week. Unless the story is set out in diary format, it's not so common to see full dates, for example, 5 July, 2011.

Genre

Usually, the genre was obvious very quickly. Whether the novel was a thriller, a romantic comedy or a crime story the first page made this clear. This wasn't so much a content element, but a style one. The genre was reflected in the style of writing.

This applies equally to short stories.

Dialogue

Not all first pages contained dialogue. First person novels, for example, were a lot less likely to need it, but I noticed that dialogue fairly often featured on a first page. From a purely visual point of view, it broke up the page and made it more inviting and easier to read, which is a very good thing for a first page. Never forget that if your agent/publisher and, ultimately, your reader doesn't like the first page, they won't read any more.

One other thing to add about dialogue is that the sooner a character speaks the sooner a reader can begin to care about him. Or not, as the case may be.

If short stories have dialogue – and 90 per cent plus do – then it's likely to be there pretty quickly, too, purely in the interests of balance.

Descriptions of characters

These weren't necessarily on the first page of a novel and they certainly weren't lengthy, but when a character was introduced, some hint of description accompanied the introduction, even when it was just a small one, such as how a character spoke, or walked.

Incidentally, generally (and there are exceptions) characters in novels are introduced by their full name, for example, Susan Henshaw. Characters in short stories don't even need to *have* a full name. Sue is fine.

As we have already seen in Chapter Five it is not necessary to give more than the briefest hint of character description in a short story, but in a novel if it's there, it has to be there quickly, and it has to be constantly but subtly reinforced.

Flashback

There is rarely any flashback on the first page of a novel

and neither should there be. I was once told by a very experienced agent that if you begin a novel and then start going backwards, you have started in the wrong place. There may be some exceptions to this rule, but generally speaking, I think this is true.

Short stories are different. It is perfectly acceptable to start with some exciting event, perhaps an argument, and then use flashback to inform the reader of previous events.

Summary

Are you feeling breathless? I was absolutely amazed at the quantity of information I found on the first pages of novels. What's more amazing still is that it has to be put there so subtly; none of it must seem contrived. It has to naturally flow, and it has to be intriguing. It's information without overload, if you like. There has to be enough to pique readers' curiosity but not so much that they're bogged down with it. The story has to be moving forward too.

The good news is that it's probably not worth worrying too much about the first page of your novel until you have completed it. In my experience, the first page I originally write for a novel is rarely the first page I end up with. Therefore it makes no sense to worry too much about it until you have completed a draft. It is pointless to edit and perfect something that you might later discard.

Interestingly, the same can apply to stories, only it's more likely to be paragraphs you cut, rather than pages. Very often, by the time you get to the end of a short story you will find that paragraph four will actually make a better beginning than paragraph one. Check this yourself next time you write a story and you'll see what I mean.

The first page of a novel - example

Just before we leave beginnings – here is a direct comparison between the first page (300 words) of a novel and the first page (300 words of a short story)

Helter Skelter by Della Galton

Vanessa Hamilton awoke to the sound of a child's laughter. Caught between the limbo of sleep and wakefulness she shoved back the duvet and sat up in the dimness of the curtained room with a smile on her face. And then reality crashed in like a punch to the heart.

She was alone, although she could still hear the murmur of voices downstairs. Saturday morning kiddies' television, she realised. Richard must have left it on. He always watched the news before he went to work. And the child's laughter had reached inside her dreams.

It had been the sweetest of dreams. She and Jennifer had been playing hide and seek in the forest. Her daughter had been running ahead of her, feet crunching over pine needles, the white material of her dress flashing between the trees.

"Wait till I say ready, Mummy. No peeking."

"No peeking," Vanessa had agreed, covering her eyes with her fingers, but leaving a gap to check Jennifer didn't wander too far from her sight.

Then she'd woken to find it wasn't real. There were no pine needles cracking underfoot, no flickering of sunlight and shadow on the forest floor, and no Jennifer, and although the reality wasn't as devastating as it had been in the early days it still hurt enough to leave her breathless.

Vanessa knew yesterday's letter from Purbeck District

81

Council had sparked it off. The letter was tucked inside a zipped compartment of her bag, but she didn't need to keep it. She knew it word for word.

'We are writing to inform you we are planning to carry out upgrades to Saint Mary's memorial garden. Disruption will be kept to a minimum, but you might want to remove any personal effects temporarily for safekeeping.'

This is not a best-selling novel (I'm sorry to say) but I hope most of the elements I've outlined above are there, that is, it has a hook, at least one character, the setting is hinted at, the genre is hinted at, and there is some description, even if it's just dialogue between the characters. Also, we know that Vanessa is a mother, or has been. There is a hint that she has lost Jennifer.

The first page of a short story - example

Here are the first 300 words of a short story. (The story was 2000 words in all).

On One Knee (published in *Woman's Weekly*)

"The thing is, Kay, you see – er – the thing is…"

She'd never seen him so nervous. "Spit it out, George." She grinned encouragingly, but it didn't seem to help.

He shifted his chair back, but it caught on the carpet and juddered so that he jolted the white-clothed table between them and she had to grab her glass of wine to stop it toppling over

"Well, you know I really like you."

"Yes." What was he doing? She'd thought he was

going to excuse himself, but instead he seemed to be disappearing under the table.

"And I think you like me too."

His voice was strangely muffled. She peered across at the space he'd vacated. He seemed to be grappling for something on the floor. Had he dropped his fork?

Suddenly he surfaced, his glasses were askew, but he'd obviously found what he was looking for.

"We rub along pretty well together," he went on, "And we've been going out for quite a while now."

Three months wasn't quite a while. Not in her book it wasn't. She'd actually been trying to cool things down a bit – he was a nice guy, but they didn't have quite as much in common as she'd thought.

Oh no. She had a sudden flash of foreboding. Surely he wasn't about to... He couldn't be... Now he was edging along the carpet on his knees towards her. His trousers made a shuffling sound, but it was probably exaggerated because the rest of the restaurant had gone so quiet.

"I'd like you to be my wife. I want to marry you, Kay. I think we're good together..."

The restaurant drew in its collective breath. He had heat in his cheeks. His ineptness made him seem extra vulnerable, extra gawky.

This story begins in dialogue, in the middle of a conversation, in fact. It's clear from the outset what's happening. The title is a bit of a clue! The setting is a restaurant although it doesn't matter where. George is proposing to a less than keen Kay. The style is gentle humour.

The story bounds along in dialogue. The main hook being is she going to say yes or no? I think we know the answer to that already. Although this could be the beginning of a novel, it's not so likely to be a novel; it's a little too brief, a little too linear, a little too lightweight.

Summary of differences

Characters are introduced in much more detail in a novel. For example, full names are used in novels. First names, or occasionally no names at all, are used in short stories.

Setting is much more critical in a novel. The reader needs a clear point of reference about where the story is set. Setting can be quite sketchy in a short story. Real place names aren't necessary although you can use them if you wish.

Hooks are needed in both, but a short story hook could be as small as a line of intriguing dialogue.

Plot – what's happening is often immediately clear in a short story. In the opening of a novel it won't necessarily be obvious. The opening must be relevant but can build more slowly. A good example of this is Jodie Picoult's novel, House Rules.

The first paragraph describes a scene which ends with the line, *'There's one single faint footprint at the threshold of the living room, pointing towards the dead body of my son, Jacob.'*

This is a brilliant hook, I'm sure you'll agree, but all is not quite as it seems. I will say no more in case you haven't read the book!

Chapter Ten
Pace – The Middle

So much for beginnings, so what happens as we progress?

What is the difference between the middle of a short story and the middle of a novel?

Depth is probably the simple answer to this question. While a short story will build rapidly towards its conclusion, carrying the reader along in its flow, a novelist will need to add depth and breadth and of course, new information, and new hooks as the story unfolds. This is done in a variety of ways.

New strands

The middle of your novel isn't a bad place to add a new strand or some new information that changes the direction of the novel. For example, if you are writing a crime novel, perhaps the police suddenly realise that their main suspect could not have committed the latest crime. Are there perhaps two murderers out there, not just one?

Complications

It's also a good place to deepen or further complicate your subplot. Perhaps you have been running a subplot that is parallel to the main plot and up until now the reader hasn't known how they touch. Maybe now is the time to link your subplot to your main plot, or perhaps to add new elements to both.

It's very easy to let the middle of a novel become flabby and filled with waffle, but if you want to keep your reader with you, you must keep it tight. Keep surprising the reader and taking your plot or characters in fresh directions and you'll avoid a flabby middle.

Structure can help you to avoid a flabby middle in a novel too. For example, you might be writing from three viewpoints and have decided to split the novel equally into three parts, so each character gets 30,000 words. So it will be your second character who has the middle section of your novel. This then, can be the place where the reader learns about how the first character's actions have impacted on her, and how this in turn causes her to do things that will affect the third character and ultimately bring the novel to a conclusion.

Don't forget the middle of a novel is a lot longer than the middle of a short story so you'll have a lot more words to play with. If you're the type of writer who plots before you start, then pay close attention to what you're going to do with the middle. If you're, like me, a plot-as-you-go, writer, then think about it carefully when you get there. Lots of novels could do with having a good pruning around the middle – which probably applies to lots of novelists too, she adds, looking at her stomach with a rueful smile!

Cliffhangers

While we're talking about the middle, I want to also touch on cliffhangers. Short stories don't have them, generally speaking, although if you were writing a particularly long story, say 3000 words upwards, then you might well have some mini cliffhangers, particularly if you were using gaps in the text for either time breaks or viewpoint changes.

Novels do and should have cliffhangers but they don't have to be massive. This is a mistake many a new novelist makes – and I'll include myself in that.

What do I mean by a massive cliffhanger?

Well, let's go back to a crime novel. Say, for example, your detective, the main character, is about to unmask the killer, she might say something like, "I know who did it. I'm going to give you his name..."

You might think this is a very handy place to end your chapter – an excellent cliffhanger in fact. You might even think it would be a fine ploy to change viewpoint in the next chapter so we (the reader) don't actually get to find out what your detective is about to say for another three or four thousand words.

You might be right. We'd certainly want to read on, wouldn't we, but ... And I'd just like to add a note of caution here, if you do this on a regular basis it could become extremely irritating.

Might your readers, instead of being intrigued and enthralled, decide to fling the book down in disgust because they are being so obviously manipulated? Some novelists do actually use the cliffhanger technique to good effect, but don't tease your reader too much, you might live to regret it.

And anyway it is not necessary. The word cliffhanger is in fact a bit of a misnomer. You really want to draw your reader in with your skilful writing, don't you? Make them want to read on because they care about your characters and what happens to them. You don't want to dangle them over a cliff on a worn out bit of old rope!

At least that's my take on the matter. By all means use cliffhangers, but don't be over dramatic. There are other, more subtle ways of enticing your reader to want more. Here are some of them:

Creating suspense without cliffhangers

Pose questions, and don't answer them too quickly.

Create suspense by giving one character information that the rest don't have. For example, give your characters secrets.

Give your reader more information than the characters have.

Have your character do things that are slightly odd, but don't give the reader an explanation until later. (Don't leave it so long that they forget though!)

Give unconnected events some commonality: for example, three women die in different countries on the same day and they are all called Eleanor. I think there might be the basis of a good thriller there – feel free to write it!

Allow your readers to think they know what's going on and then throw in an event which reverses their expectations.

Summary of differences

Whether you are writing a novel or a short story the middle is perhaps the hardest part and the easiest place to get it wrong.

The middle of a short story should deepen both plot and characterisation and should drive the story forward to its conclusion.

The middle of a novel should do the same, but there's a lot more room – so it will also need new information, possibly new twists, subplots and characters.

Short stories don't have cliffhangers as a rule.

Novels do have cliffhangers but they need to be used with skill and precision. Don't rely too heavily on cliffhangers for suspense.

Chapter Eleven
Pace – The End

So let's have a look at the ends of short stories and novels. If you've read my book *How to Write and Sell Short Stories,* you will know that I find writing the beginnings of short stories quite easy. I could write them all day. But writing the ends of short stories is a different matter, it's by far the hardest part.

Interestingly, I find that this works in reverse in novels. Writing the beginning of a novel is difficult. For one thing, so much has to be in them, as we have seen in Chapter Nine. Writing the end of a novel is much more straightforward because everything else in the novel has been leading to that point.

It may be different for you. So let's look at this in a bit more detail. There are many similarities between the two forms. What kind of ending can short stories have?

The twist.
The surprise ending.
The straight ending.
The poignant ending.
The open ending.

I've probably missed some. But basically the endings of novels are much the same.

Twist endings

In a short story the twist will be very close to the end, if not the last line, or the last word. If you're using a twist in a novel, the twist will also be very close to the end. Otherwise, it wouldn't be a twist!

But whereas in a story the twist might hang on the last word, in a novel it's much more likely to be on the last page, or perhaps the last paragraph. It won't be quite as sudden. Although I'm sure there are exceptions to this rule!

Surprise endings

The surprise ending in a novel is probably going to be rather more leisurely. Having said this, the last page of a novel must have some impact. If you have a surprise ending on page 350 and your novel goes on for another 10 pages then you must have a good reason or you're in danger of your ending falling flat.

Straight endings

In this type of ending, there is no big twist, no real surprises, just a conclusion, which is often dramatic. Think disaster movie endings: the baddie gets caught; the world gets saved; the hero gets the woman. Or the heroine gets the man.

They are perhaps the hardest endings to pull off effectively on the page. I think this applies to short stories as well as to novels. But if you are going towards an inevitable or straight ending you should make sure your last line has some kind of resonance – perhaps it echoes back to something earlier in the novel.

Also, bear in mind that most endings have some kind of surprise element, even if it's just a very small surprise after the main action is over. Or perhaps, although you have tied up most of the loose ends, you have left one tiny unresolved detail until the last line. Please don't feel you have to tie up all the loose ends in a novel by the way. You don't – unlike a short story where it's more common. But it's nice to leave the reader with a small surprise. I once heard an agent refer to this as the after eight mint effect, which struck me as very apt, because it leaves a nice taste in the reader's mouth.

Epilogues

I should just mention epilogues, which don't apply to short stories, but which you may want to use in your novel.

They are a useful device for catching up with your characters in the future, for example, your novel might end with your character getting pregnant, or landing her man, and the epilogue skips forward to the time when the baby is born, or she actually marries him. I think I've done that in the wrong order, haven't I!

However, don't use an epilogue unless it's absolutely necessary. It's not necessary, or even desirable, to tie up every loose end. Not tying up loose ends can also leave open the option of writing a sequel if the novel does well.

Poignant endings

Poignant endings mean just that – they are poignant – and I think they are handled very similarly in both short stories and novels.

They tend to underline what the story or novel has

been about, but they also add something new, something thought provoking. One of the best poignant endings I've read lately was that of the *The Boy in the Striped Pyjamas*, written by John Boyne. I challenge you to read it and not weep.

Open endings

As the name suggests, these are the type of endings which are left open, so in effect there is no definite ending.

These can work brilliantly, or they can be so obscure that the reader doesn't have a clue what actually happened. Whether you use them in a short story or a novel, be very careful yours doesn't fall into the latter category.

An open ending should *not*, contrary to what some authors seem to think, leave the reader hanging in mid air wondering if there are any more pages. It should make you think and it should at the very least offer possibilities about what has happened. An open ending means that readers make up their minds about what has happened, having been given more than one option to consider, but the author should probably know what has happened. The writer is just toying with the reader a little.

One of the best examples I've read of a novel with an open ending is *Wish You Were Here* by Lesley Grant Adamson. It still sticks in my mind despite the fact I read it over fifteen years ago. It's about a woman who goes on holiday and gets picked up by a serial killer. The focus of the novel is: will she find out in time, or won't she?

I'm not going to tell you how it ends, in case you want to read it for yourself, suffice to say, it's absolutely chilling and I loved it. And I still haven't quite decided what happened, although I do contemplate it occasionally.

Cliffhanger endings

For obvious reasons these don't apply to short stories, or they shouldn't. I have never seen one that works anyway, but they can be used in novels, usually if the novel is part of a series. If it isn't, then a cliffhanger ending would be very annoying. In fact, even if the novel is part of a series they can be annoying so use them with care. It is possible to 'finish' a novel and still have enough of a cliffhanger to make the reader want to go on reading. Some publishers will print the first chapter of the author's next book in the back of their current one. This also seems a good idea to me. Authors then have two chances to entice their readers to buy the next book.

The last page

So what should be on the last page of a novel? This is not quite as simple as what should be on the first page of a novel, as naturally it will depend on what has gone before. There are no fixed rules here, although you should be bringing your main storyline to a satisfying conclusion however you interpret that for your particular novel.

As we've already discussed there are various types of endings for both short stories and novels, but let's just finish this section by looking at some differences when it comes to the last pages of novels and short stories.

Summary of differences

You don't need to tie up every loose end in a novel, but you probably will in a short story.

Epilogues are only used in long fiction, not short.

Cliffhangers are not used to end short stories, but can occasionally be used to good effect in novels.

In a novel, although you're ending your story, it's good to leave your readers wanting more. And, as I've already mentioned, I don't mean they should be looking for another page, I mean they should put the book down and regret that they've come to the end of it. If you can leave them with that feeling of regret that they've finished your book, then with luck they will go out and buy the next one.

Chapter Twelve
Structure and Flashback

Using flashback

Flashback is used in fiction to show the reader events which happened before the story started. These events will have some impact on what is taking place currently in the story.

Handling flashback in the short story

When you use flashback in a short story you'll need to indicate to the reader that it's going to begin and then indicate at some later point that the flashback is going to finish, that is, you'll need links both in to flashback and out of it again. You need to move the reader smoothly in to and out of the past.

While you're actually in the flashback you can treat it as though it's happening in the 'now' of the novel, i.e. you can write it scenically. There is no need to use the pluperfect tense.

This is the beginning of a short story, which opens in the present, but goes quite quickly into flashback. It's called, *Going Back to Whitney,* published in *My Weekly.*

Seagulls circled overhead as Kay carried her suit carrier and rucksack across the car park. The Mariner had been done up. She could smell fresh paint as she pushed open the door and there was a new fake-wood floor.

A lad who didn't look old enough to be serving gave her the key to her room. "I'll get someone to show you up."

"Don't worry – I used to work here." She smiled at his surprised expression, wanting to add, "Before you were born." But it hadn't been quite that long.

It was only as she closed the door of room 14 behind her and unpacked her weekend clothes that she allowed herself to think of Pete.

This last sentence is a hint to the reader that we'll shortly be going into flashback. We then go on:

He might not live in Whitney any more, but she sensed he would. He was a homebody, that's what her mother had said when they'd first started going out, the type who'd marry a local girl and have her children and never really go far from his roots.

The section that follows is the actual lead-in to flashback – note how we start in the pluperfect tense with the word, 'He'd ...' We stay in the pluperfect tense for a few lines just to clarify the time change.

He'd been halfway along that path when they'd met. He'd been engaged to a girl called Maggie, although Kay hadn't known that straight away.

She'd met Pete at a party. They'd bumped arms as they were getting drinks from the table in the crowded kitchen. The force of the jolt caused him to spill his.

"Sorry," she'd said.

"Don't be."

She'd looked up into amused dark eyes.

(Now we change into standard past tense)

Not many men were taller than her. They were close enough for her to smell the shampoo in his unruly hair and see the little chip in his front tooth when he smiled.
"Pete Lacey."

"Kay." She felt as though she were giving him so much more than just her name.

"Shall we go somewhere a bit quieter?"

They moved to the less crowded back room where the music wasn't as loud. And she remembered that right from that first moment no one else had existed.

They talked about music and food and where they'd grown up – her parents lived in West Arlington, his were here in the village – and what they hoped to do with their lives. He wanted to work in his father's garage. She wanted to travel.

About an hour after they'd met he mentioned Maggie with a flicker of guilt in his eyes.

"She isn't here then?" Kay glanced around in alarm, half expecting to see a jealous girlfriend bearing down on them.

"No, she's seeing a friend."

"I see." Suddenly aware there was barely a gap between their thighs on the sofa she moved her leg.

He moved his back.

"We're just talking," he said. "Maggie isn't the possessive type."

She would have been worried though, Kay thought, because no way was this going to stay 'just talking'.

He kept touching her: her arm, her shoulder, nowhere he shouldn't, but everywhere he made contact her skin remembered his fingers.

They spent that first night together. It was the type of party where everyone stayed over, wrapped in sleeping bags or chatting around the kitchen table, getting steadily mellower – the sort of party teenagers had when their parents were away.

They had the sofa. They both remained fully clothed. They didn't even kiss, but Kay leant her head back against his denim-clad shoulder and he stroked her hair.

She had never felt so at peace with anyone before. So at peace and yet with an undercurrent of excitement as if something huge was opening up before them.

In the morning they went their separate ways, but not before he caught her hand.

"I have to see you again."

"What about Maggie?" She'd known even then it was a half hearted protest because she had to see him again too.

(It's only when the flashback is almost over that we remind the reader we're actually in the past by the use of the words in the above section, 'She'd known even then...'

After that there is actually a break shown by a row of stars (see below) before we inform the reader that we're back in the present.

Her mobile rang and Kay unburied it from her bag, re-joining the present with a little sigh.

The example above is a standard way of introducing flashback in a short story and then bringing the reader back into the present once more.

As you can see, it happened fairly quickly in the short

story, the first page in fact. This is fine too. Things are slightly different in a novel.

Handling flashback in the novel

As I've already mentioned, it is not a good plan to use flashback, particularly a large chunk of it, on the first page of a novel. However, there's no reason why you shouldn't use mini flashbacks elsewhere. These are handled in much the same way.

This is an example of a mini flashback in my novel, *Helter Skelter*. Vanessa, the main character, is telling Tracey, who she works with, what it was like to be brought up on a fairground.

"What did Izzy do at the fair?" Tracey asked.

"All sorts. She had a coconut shy and a juvenile ride. And for a long time, she had the Helter Skelter. Me and Garrin used to drive her mad. We used to pour cooking oil down the slide so we could get a bit of speed up. In those days we used to go down it on those old woven mats. Garrin used to carve bits off them to make them more aerodynamic."

Up to now we've been in dialogue, but the next line alerts the reader to the fact we're about to go into flashback. As does the use of the word, *"She'd ..."*

Vanessa smiled at the memory. She'd loved the Helter Skelter when she was small: the creaky old stairs, with gaps where you could look through and see the grass far below; the rhythmic beat of the music and the smell of fried onions and burgers; then the stomach crunching moment when you pushed off the top and the breathless slide downwards. More often than not, Garrin would be waiting for her at the bottom, arms outstretched so they tumbled onto the ground together laughing.

For a moment she ached for the simple pleasures of times gone by. It was an effort to pull herself together and continue the story.

"One of Izzy's husbands had the Paratrooper."

This is a mini flashback, a tiny visual snapshot of the past, which ends with the line, *'For a moment she ached...* We are actually mid conversation between two characters, but it could easily have been a little longer than it is.

So, as you can see, the techniques for using flashback in novels and short stories are much the same, but you have a lot more scope when it comes to novels. Mainly because you have so much more space. Let's look at some of the ways that using flashback is different in novels.

Using chapters to introduce flashback

Chapters are very useful devices for jumping around in time. You may, for example, want to have the first three or four chapters of your novel in the current time, and then have chapters five and six in some past time, which sheds light on what is happening in the present. For example, your character may have a very turbulent relationship with her brother, and this is the main conflict of your novel, so at some point you may wish to whisk the reader back to their childhood to show us the beginnings of this rocky relationship.

Or the seed of your conflict may go back several generations and you may want to take the reader into the distant past. This can easily be achieved by devoting whole chapters to the past. Chapters can be headed up with dates to make sure the reader is clear which time period they are in. In fact, if you're going to do this a lot then dates can be very helpful. As long as you make it clear which time period you're taking the reader back to, you don't need to be consecutive either. But don't just dart around in time without good reason. Or you will end up with a very confused reader. Time was used to brilliant effect in Audrey Niffenegger's novel, *The Time Traveller's Wife*.

A simpler structure might just be alternating chapters. I once read a crime novel about a robbery, which alternated between what was happening now and the events in the past that had led up to this point. It took the reader easily backwards and forwards, chapter by chapter.

This doesn't just have to be done by time. You might wish to transport your reader back and forth via different characters' viewpoints.

When should I introduce flashback?

The answer to this is whenever it's necessary, with one big proviso. Don't introduce it on the first page of your novel. Short stories are different. You can introduce it whenever you like. It is common to see flashback used on the first page of a short story.

Handling back story

Back story is slightly different to flashback. It means introducing facts about your characters or plot that haven't been shown in your story in real time.

You might want to let your reader know how two characters had met, for example, without taking the reader into a full flashback scene. Or you might want to let the reader know your character is terribly afraid of horses or spiders or was bullied in the past.

You may be planning a big scene in which your main character is going to come face to face with a loose horse and the scene will have a great deal more impact if we know that he or she is terrified of horses. If you are going to set up this type of scenario you will need to weave your back story about her fear of horses in before the big confrontational scene.

You can't just plonk it in the previous chapter. In order for it to be fully effective it's a seed that will need to be sown earlier on in the novel, and the reader reminded of it once or twice before we get to the big scene.

Sowing seeds

In some ways this is the essence of novel writing. The earlier chapters of a novel are a lot about sowing seeds of information that will grow throughout the novel and ultimately flower. While this is also done, to a very minor extent, in short-story writing, it's a big part of novel writing.

What are the pitfalls of using flashback and back story?

I think there are two possible problems writers encounter when using either flashback or back story.

The first is that readers will lose interest if they are forced to move into a different time zone. This applies equally to short stories and novels. Let's assume something very exciting is happening in the present, and you decide to take your readers away from it and into flashback to an event that happened in the past. It's important to swiftly engage readers in the flashback scene, or there is a danger they will stop reading. You will have the same problem when you bring the reader back into the present – the now of the novel – again.

The other problem that can arise is confusion. If you move readers around too often and you don't do it skilfully enough, there is a danger they will be so confused they won't know where – or rather 'when' they are. And they might also stop reading.

Either of the above problems can be resolved with skilful writing. If you're taking your readers away from a gripping scene, you need to swiftly engage them in another one. Make sure you always signpost flashback clearly in and out – and don't do it too often.

So let's move on to structure.

How does short story structure and novel structure differ?

Structure and its use in fiction is a subject that's always interested me. All fiction, and non-fiction come to that, needs some kind of structure. More often than not the structure of a short story or novel is invisible. But let's just take a look at some of the more visible structures.

Types of structure

Diary

As you'd expect this is when the story is told via diary extracts. They crop up regularly in short stories and novels. For the latter, think *Bridget Jones' Diary* by Helen Fielding or *The Diary of a Young Girl* by Anne

Frank. Using a diary structure enables the writer to manipulate time very easily. The problem of having to progress through periods of time when nothing exciting is happening is solved as your character only ever needs to make interesting and relevant diary entries.

Time

A diary structure involves time, but there are many other structures that also involve time. For example you could write your story using any of the following time formats:

Months of the year.
Days of the year (tricky in a short story).
Hours of the day.
One day. (Think David Nicholls)
Day and night (alternating).
Seasons.

There are infinite varieties. Most of the time structures can be used for both short stories and novels.

Letters

This is when a story is told in the form of either one letter or a series of letters between characters.

It's possible to write a short story using either one letter or several. Most novels, for obvious reasons, will need more than one letter. They don't have to be letters in the traditional sense, texts and emails could be included.

Double Handers

These are stories told using more than one viewpoint.

They are often split into sections, each section belonging to a different character. Often the different characters' viewpoints are headed up with their names. You can use as many characters as you like, but more than three can be confusing in a short story.

Actually, I think more than three or four may also be too much for a novel, although you do sometimes see novels where each chapter is told via a different character's viewpoint. I'm not sure you should attempt the latter as a first novel, unless you have a really powerful plot that will hold your characters together.

There's a danger when you have too many viewpoints that the reader will be interested in some of the characters' viewpoints, but not all of them, and the more characters there are, the greater that risk is.

More Unusual Structures

When you're writing a short story you can use words or objects as a structure. For example, I once wrote a story called *Rain*. There were five sections and each section began with the sentence 'It's raining.'

Using words as a structure is probably a little bit too subtle for a novel, especially if the sections are long. The reader isn't likely to notice the connection – unless your words are particularly memorable!

You could use memorable events though. Perhaps each section could start with a wedding, or a funeral. Or possibly, in the case of crime fiction, a murder!

Summary of differences

Flashback can be used on the first page of short stories, but it's not advisable to use it on the first page of a novel.

It's much easier to play with time in a novel than it is in a short story.

Other devices such as viewpoint can be used in conjunction with flashback in a novel. This is not possible with short stories.

Most structures can be used in both short and long fiction, but the more subtle the structure is, the less likely it is to work in a novel.

Chapter Thirteen
Using a Theme

What is a theme?

I think about themes as being the focus of what I'm writing. A theme can usually be boiled down to one word: forgiveness; revenge; loss; loneliness; fear; class; love. Take your pick, there are hundreds. I find they are very helpful to a writer because they can keep you on track, help you decide which parts of your writing are relevant and which need to be cut.

Using a theme in a short story

We're all familiar with using a theme in a short story. Many writing competitions are themed, for example, write a story using the theme hope, or jealousy, or revenge. And you'll probably agree that they're quite helpful too. A theme instantly focuses the mind. If someone says write a story, any subject, any length, my mind goes blank.

However, if someone says write a story on the theme of hope I could instantly think of two or three possible scenarios involving hope.

So we're accustomed to using themes in short stories, but is it the same with novels?

Using a theme in a novel

Perhaps in some ways it is the same. After all, many novels fall into genres, don't they? So is theme the same as genre? No, I don't think it is. You could for example, have a crime novel where the theme was vengeance. Or a chick lit novel where the theme was forgiveness. I think theme is more specific than genre. It's also a bit more subconscious. Not all writers start off with the intention of using a theme, but many do. And interestingly many writers use the same theme or themes over and over again in their fiction.

I think that's because writing comes from deep within us. It's affected by our experiences of the world – it has to be. So there's a good chance you are going to use a theme whether you like it or not. Therefore, it makes sense to be aware of it. That way, it can help you to write too.

Is it necessary to have a theme in what I'm writing?

Maybe not, but I think a theme is a writer's friend. It can help hugely in the editing process, as I've mentioned. And if you're a plotter it could help in the planning process too. Many writers start with a theme and go from there.

If you use mind maps to plot, you could try writing down your theme in the centre of a page and then exploring different interpretations of that theme. In this way you can develop subplots that are linked to your main plot by theme.

How can a theme help?

I also find it helpful to know what my story, whether it's short or long, is about. I've written several novels, although, at the time of writing, only two of them have been published. Chronologically, they are novels, numbers four and five.

My first three were 'practice novels'.

So, let's go back a bit. I wrote my first novel, which was called *Prisoners*, when I was about 22. It was a about a woman who works in a pet shop and falls in love with someone she shouldn't (her married boss). There are a few animal characters and they have a few nights out (the people, not the animals) and in the end the couple get it together.

If this sounds like an immense muddle, then that's because it was. I knew nothing about writing novels, or that much about writing anything, when I penned it. I'd had four or five short stories published when I wrote *Prisoners*. I thought writing a novel was simply a matter of writing 60,000 words. (That was the required word count in those days.)

Moving swiftly on, my first published novel, *Passing Shadows*, was about a woman who works in an animal sanctuary and falls in love with someone she shouldn't (the father of her best friend's child.) There are a few animal characters and they have a few nights out (the people, not the animals) and in the end the couple get it together.

Sounds familiar doesn't it? So why did this novel work and *Prisoners* not work? Well, partly because I knew a bit more about what I was doing. *Passing Shadows* had a plot and a subplot too, as it happens. But I also think having a theme helped me a lot.

Incidentally, don't feel you have to stick to just one theme. Lots of themes are so interconnected that it's hard to separate them.

Prisoners had no theme, well, perhaps it did – there's a big clue in the title, isn't there? But I didn't know how to develop themes in those days.

Passing Shadows does have a theme. In fact, it has more than one. They are abandonment, second chances (I know that's two words, not one), redemption, and of course love.

The entire novel is about getting a second chance at love. In fact, it was originally called *Love and Second Chances*. Incidentally, that's a good title tip – theme and title are strongly linked.

Passing Shadows opens with Maggie, a vet nurse, rescuing a red kite that has a broken wing. (Thematically, she is giving the bird a second chance.) One of the subplots in this novel involves a character whose wife ran away with his best friend. (He gets a second chance at love.)

I'm not going to dissect every scene, but I'm aware that they all echo the themes and so do the subplots.

Incidentally, I didn't sit down and write every scene with my theme in my mind. As I've already said, it's on a much more subconscious level than that. Sometimes your theme will emerge while you're writing. You suddenly realise what your novel is about. That can be a wonderful eureka moment. And it's also a great editing tool.

Try playing a game with well known films. See if you can work out any of the themes. For example I was thinking about Alfred Hitchcock's *Psycho* once and it struck me that apart from its more obvious themes of identity and corruption, the theme of theft also crops up regularly.

It starts with a robbery, doesn't it. Marion Crane (Janet Leigh) steals some money from her employers in order to start a new life. Norman Bates subsequently steals her life when he murders her in the shower. He has also stolen his mother's identity. Taxidermy (his hobby) is also a form of theft, and, just as he keeps the bodies of wild creatures, so he keeps his own mother's body.

Just for fun, next time you're watching a film, see if you can work out what the themes are and then see if you can see them in action in specific scenes. A good theme can underpin every single scene in a film or novel, whether the author intended it to or not! It really is fascinating stuff.

Incidentally, I've noticed that script writers do this too. While they might have several plot lines running in a soap like *Coronation Street*, for example, there is often a common theme underpinning them, such as, loss or pride or jealousy.

I frequently tell people I only watch soaps for research – and it's true, as you can see. I am merely looking for interlinking themes!

Can I use the same theme for a novel and a short story?

Yes, absolutely. Themes are so generic. It really is simply a matter of how far you want to develop them.

Summary of differences

Themes can be used with great effect in both short and long fiction.

They can be used as a plotting aid, and in novels are useful as a subplotting aid.

The main difference here is when you're editing. Editing

a short story is a relatively straightforward matter, as we'll see in the next chapter.

But if you know what your theme is when you are editing your novel, then you can use it as a yardstick as to what to keep and what to cut. Ask yourself the question: does this scene echo my theme? It may be enough to help you decide what's relevant and what's not.

Chapter Fourteen
Editing and Revision

Editing is something we are all familiar with, but there are some big differences when it comes to editing short stories and novels. Mainly the differences arise because of the huge difference in length between the two forms. In this chapter I want to discuss some of the problems I encountered when I began to edit my novels and the solutions I found.

Editing a short story

It's relatively simple to edit a short story. It's not very long – one or two thousand words – so it can be done in one sitting. Here are some of the things I look for when I'm editing:

Opening sentence – is it good enough?
Repetition and superfluous words
Clumsy sentences
An overuse of adverbs/adjectives
Things that don't make sense
Have I inadvertently changed a character's name or eye colour?
Have I given enough clues for the end if it's a twist?
Is the dialogue doing its job?
Do my characters have different voices?

Is there enough/too much setting?
Is the end too obvious/obscure/weak?

I'm sure this isn't an exhaustive list, but you get the picture. And I would also do all of the above when I'm editing a novel. However, I found there were some significant differences when I began to edit novels.

Editing a novel

Continuity was one of the first differences I noticed. Of course, you need continuity when you're editing a short story too, but it's fairly easy to achieve when you don't have many words. You can simply glance back at the text to see what you've already said. To illustrate, I'm just going to pick one item from the list above?

Have I inadvertently changed a character's name or eye colour?

You're unlikely to change your main character's name inadvertently (I hope) because you know them so well. But it's very easy to change minor characters' names or appearances because they are possibly not so clearly defined in your mind, and also because there might well be long gaps between the times they appear. It's quite easy, for example, to make a minor character very softly-spoken the first time they appear, and then forget all about that aspect of him when he comes back into the novel later.

To get round this particular problem I keep a plain postcard for each of my characters which lists all their details, how they speak, walk, act – and also holds a photograph of them, which helps. I don't write visually, but if I have a picture I can refer to (these are cut out from magazines/catalogues/newspapers etc.), I find it's much easier. If you do this as you write, it will save you a lot of time later.

While we're on the subject of continuity, I once had a character going out for dinner for the evening and then coming home and having a pizza. (This was in my first novel, *Prisoners*.)

"Was she particularly hungry?" a writer friend asked when she read it through for me.

No, she wasn't. But she went out for dinner in Chapter Four and she didn't get home until Chapter Eight, by which time I'd forgotten I'd ever sent her out for dinner in the first place. Several thousand words separated the two meals, if not actual real time in the novel. This is another problem that's unlikely to happen in a short story because of the much shorter timescale.

Using a chapter overview

To get around this problem I have a system for novel writing. I create an overview of my novel, which I fill in as I write. Here's an example – on the next page is a chapter overview for *Helter Skelter*.

What happens	Number of words	Time of year	Viewpoint used
Chapter One Vanessa realises her husband, Richard, of 8 years is deceiving her. She leaves to go in search of her fairground past (prompted by a letter regarding her daughter's grave.)	2144	June	Vanessa
Chapter Two Garrin gives Amanda a riding lesson. When she falls off, he bullies her into remounting.	1363	July	Garrin
Chapter Three Garrin visits Izzy and realises he bullied Amanda because she reminds him of Vanessa.	1954	Same	Garrin
Chapter Four Vanessa drives to fairground, finds it gone and realises extent of Richard's deception. Goes to Jennifer's grave.	2814	Same	Vanessa

This system has several purposes. It means I can keep track of important events that have happened in the novel. I wouldn't, for example, forget my main character had already eaten!

It also means I can make sure something did actually happen. Sometimes I get carried away and write lots of words where nothing 'really' happens or I repeat information that's already been given because I am in a different character's viewpoint.

It means I can keep track of time in the novel. This is particularly important if you're not writing chapters in chronological order.

It means I can keep track of viewpoint – and makes sure the main characters do have most of the viewpoint.

It means I can keep track of chapter lengths.

Cutting without losing continuity

Another problem I found with editing novels is that it's quite easy to cut something out of a novel which relates to something else further on, or further back, and then forget it's gone. You know you've written it; therefore the information is in your head, even if it's no longer in the text.

For example, I may decide when I've finished writing a novel that I need to cut Chapter Six entirely, because it's repetitious, but what if in doing so I also cut out facts that are needed? There are bound to be some. To get round this, I don't actually delete Chapter Six, I transfer it to a new file, called Bits of ... (insert title of novel).

I can do this, secure in the knowledge that I can refer to the now deleted chapter and make sure that any relevant information goes into the novel in some other guise. I have found this incredibly useful.

Cooling-off periods

If you've substantially altered your work, whether it's short or long fiction I'd advise you to have a cooling-off period before you do the final draft.

If it's a short story this can be a day or two. I urge you to leave it a lot longer if it's a novel. I'm talking about the final draft here by the way. By all means edit the last chapter you've written just before you write the next.

Final edits

So how do I know when I've done the final edits? This is a question I often get asked and the answer is that the final edits should really only be a matter of checking punctuation or altering the odd word. If you're doing any substantial edits, for example, adding new scenes, you will need a further cooling-off period. If you don't have one, you are likely to leave mistakes in your final draft.

This might sound like an obvious thing to say but the fewer mistakes there are in your final draft the better. I've been working as an editor for the past two years (as well as a writer) and I've read hundreds of submission. They are presumably the final drafts we get sent, but it's often hard to tell. Obvious mistakes on the first page of a manuscript mark out the writer as an amateur.

Flawless manuscripts at least tell us that the writer is a professional, even if we don't go on to publish their work.

Proof reading

Proof reading is slightly different again. You might also want to do a proof reading check before you send your manuscript off into the big wide world for others to peruse. Personally, I always do these on paper. I work on a computer most of the time but I don't do on-screen proof reads because I think I will miss things.

When I am doing my final proof reading – and this is before a publisher gets involved, I print off the manuscript and then I check it line by line, holding a ruler underneath the text to make sure there are no mistakes. If this sounds like hard work, that's because it is, but I think it's worth it.

Writing is an incredibly competitive business. I want my work to be as perfect as it can be before I send it out into the fray.

Summary of differences

Don't delete anything permanently from your computer. As well as keeping previous drafts of novels, also keep anything you remove from subsequent drafts in a document linked (by title) to the novel document that you can easily find.

It's not usually necessary to keep every single sentence that's ever been in a short story! Although you might want to keep various drafts if they are different lengths because they may be suitable for different markets.

A short story won't need as long a cooling-off period after its final edits as a novel.

Do the final edits for both on paper if you want to be sure you haven't missed anything.

Chapter Fifteen
Finding the Best Title

What's the main difference between titles for novels and titles for short stories?

This was a question I didn't give any serious consideration to until I wrote a novel. In fact I wasn't sure there even was a difference until my publisher told me she wasn't keen on the title I'd picked for my first novel and asked me to suggest some different ones.

One or twice she said, "No, that's more of a short story title." And it was only then that I started thinking there might be a difference. But what was it?

Perhaps it's a question of size. Novels are a lot bigger than short stories and maybe they need a title to reflect this. I don't mean you should use a title for your novel that is lengthy (although these can work well). I mean that you should think big in terms of words. Consider the following two lists:

Atonement	Rain
Addiction	Shoes
Sisters	Lost
Mercy	Buzzwords
Secrets	Priorities

As I'm sure you've gathered, the ones on the left are the titles of novels and the ones on the right are the titles of short stories. And yes, some of them could be interchangeable. But generally novel titles are bigger, more all-encompassing, and they hint at big subjects. I can envisage a whole novel that's about atonement, but I find it harder to envisage a whole novel that's about rain.

Here are some multi word titles:

Bloody Valentine	Dancing Shoes
The God Delusion	The Gold Peg
Trick of the Dark	A Twist of Fate
Wild Justice	Mr Fixit
Life of Pi	A Touch of Romance

Once again, the ones on the left are the titles of novels and the ones on the right are the titles of short stories and again, there are some interchangeable ones. I could see *Trick of the Dark* as a short story title too, and I could possibly see *A Twist of Fate* as a novel title. But I couldn't see *The Gold Peg* as a novel title, any more than I could see *The God Delusion* as a short story title. So I hope you will see that there is a difference.

Bear in mind that titles go in and out of fashion. It has been fashionable to have very specific titles, for example: *A Short History of Tractors in Ukrainian* or *The Curious Incident of the Dog in the Night-Time.* It may not be fashionable by the time this book is published. So do check what's in the bestseller lists.

But here are some tips on finding a good title whatever you write.

Think theme

Think about your theme – one word titles tend to echo the theme, which is why they can work for either short or long fiction.

Be specific and be unusual

The more specific a title the more interesting it is. I am not especially interested in either the history of tractors or the Ukraine, but I could not resist *A Short History of Tractors in Ukrainian* as a title.

The Girl with the Dragon Tattoo is also a very evocative title. As is *The Boy in the Striped Pyjamas*. These titles are also visual. You'll instantly have a picture in your head. I think you'll agree that they're much more interesting than general titles like, *Fields*, or *Dreams*, or *Memories*. Not that there's anything wrong with these titles – if they're extremely relevant, but imagine that you're standing in a book shop surrounded by hundreds of titles, or flicking through an ebook store.

Which title is going to catch your attention – *Dreams* or *The Girl with the Dragon Tattoo?*

Be provocative

Being slightly provocative never hurts. *The God Delusion* is a good example of this, I think. Whatever your beliefs it certainly sticks in your mind. And this is definitely one of the things a good title should do.

Finding titles for a series

You might, of course, be planning to write a series of

novels or a series of short stories, in which case your titles are even more important.

Let's talk novels for a moment. If you can come up with a sufficiently brilliant idea then the rest of the work is easy. Sue Grafton springs to mind with her series, *A is for Alibi, B is for Burglar* etc.

Other writers use stylistic devices, for example, all their books will have one word titles, or two word titles.

Or they might have one overall title and each book in the series will have an individual title.

If you're writing a series or anthology of short stories it might be slightly easier – as you could list them under one main title, which gives the theme for the whole series, for example, *Cat Tails*, or *Vampire Nights*, or *Girl's Night In*.

Whatever you are writing you should put a great deal of thought into your title. It is one of the things that will help to sell your story, both to an editor, which is vital if you want to get published, and later to a reader.

Test your title

Finally, and again this is just for fun, you might want to test the effectiveness of your title using an internet based scoring system like Lulu Titlescorer. *www.lulu.com/titlescorer*

All you have to do is input your proposed title, along with some facts about it, and the test will determine what chance your novel has of becoming a bestseller – based on the title alone. Food for thought!

Summary of differences

For novel titles, think big. Think high concept.

For both think about using unusual words or combinations of words.

Bear in mind that very long titles may not fit on a book spine.

Don't be too general for either novel or short story titles.

Echoing your theme in your title is helpful for both short and long fiction.

Chapter Sixteen
The Synopsis and the Blurb

Writing a synopsis for a novel

This book is about making the transition between short stories and novels and one of the traditionally big differences is that if you plan to become a novelist, you will need to know how to write a synopsis.

Publishers and agents have all sorts of different requirements as to what they require in length and detail. Check with them before you begin. If you're sending your submission package (usually three chapters and a synopsis) to more than one agent or publisher you might well have to do several different versions of your synopsis.

Generally speaking though, they will want a brief overview of your novel. This is usually about one page, single spaced. The purpose of the synopsis is to tell them what your book is about. It is not to tell them about every single plot twist and turn. The best definition I've come across of a synopsis is, a summary of your novel, with feeling.

Why do publishers need one?

Most publishers haven't got time to read the entire novel in the first instance. They ask for the first three chapters, which show them how you write, and a synopsis, which tells them what the novel is about and that there is enough plot to sustain the novel's length.

What length should it be?

Lengths vary from publisher to publisher, so check this, but the current trend is towards a shorter synopsis, about 1000 words for a 90,000 word novel. Some agents will ask for a one page synopsis, which is even shorter.

How should I present it?

The synopsis should be typed in single line spacing unless the publisher specifies differently. It should also be written in third person and in present tense.

Do I have to give away the end?

Yes, you do, which is why it's so hard to write a good synopsis.

What else should be included?

Your synopsis should introduce your MAIN characters and MAIN scenes. It should tell the publisher where the novel is set and what it is about. It does not have to include minor characters, although it might include a subplot. It might also include the theme of your novel. You can if you wish highlight the names of the main characters as you introduce them.

An example of a novel synopsis

This is the synopsis for my novel, *Helter Skelter*

Helter Skelter is a contemporary love story set in a show jumping yard on the beautiful Purbeck coast.

Being a suburban wife and working for her husband's business is a far cry from the life **Vanessa Hamilton** once had, growing up and working in a fair. During the five years of her marriage to property developer, **Richard** she hasn't seen **Aunt Izzy** who brought her up, **Nanna Kane**, who owned the fairground, or **Garrin Tate**, the man she was desperately in love with until tragedy tore them apart. Vanessa gave birth to a stillborn baby, **Jennifer**.

When Vanessa receives a letter from the council advising her they are planning upgrades to the memorial garden where Jennifer is buried, she tells Richard she needs to go back. He tries to dissuade her – having always insisted she cut the ties of the past – and they argue. Anxious to make up she visits him at work and is stunned to see him kiss his business partner, **Tara Jacobs**.

Needing time to think Vanessa drives to Knollsea and is shocked to find a block of flats on the fairground site. She learns that Nanna Kane died shortly after she left, leaving the fairground to her grandson, Garrin. She also discovers the land was bought and developed by her husband's firm. Furious and upset at Richard's deception, she tracks Garrin down to the yard where he trains both horses and people and has established a reputation as a brilliant, but ruthless instructor. He also bought Izzy, who he has always been close to, a house nearby. They share an ambition to jump his horse, Derry, at the Horse of the Year Show. Derry was bred from a mare belonging to Izzy's uncle – Izzy's background is horses.

Garrin has not forgiven Vanessa and is not pleased to see her. However, they do spend a passionate night together. The following morning he tells her to leave and Vanessa realises, too late, that he was motivated not by love, but revenge.

She returns home to confront Richard, who denies he is having an affair and says he didn't tell her about Nanna Kane to protect her. Vanessa doesn't believe him and asks for a divorce. But he refuses to listen and flies to Spain on business.

While Richard is in Spain Vanessa discovers she is pregnant. She now knows she is still in love with Garrin and dreams he will soften towards her when he finds out she is carrying their child.

At first it seems she is right. Garrin allows her to stay at Fair Winds. Then Richard arrives and tells Vanessa the baby could be his – although he's always said he cannot father children. He offers to take her back, saying he will accept the baby as his own. Vanessa refuses, but she doesn't tell Garrin, and although Richard leaves her alone, all through her pregnancy, the time bomb of the paternity test hangs over her.

When Vanessa's daughter, **Isobel**, is born, Richard delights in telling Garrin the child is his. Garrin is devastated that Vanessa has betrayed him again. Later, when Isobel is proved to be Garrin's child, he tells Vanessa he will apply for custody. He also finds solace in the company of one of his students, **Amanda Battersby-Smythe**.

Richard, still furious that Vanessa refuses to go back to him, kidnaps Isobel in order to force Vanessa back to their marital home. Garrin, believing she has gone of her own free will, won't listen to explanations and Vanessa moves out with Isobel, determined to forget him.

Richard later tells Vanessa there was no chance of him ever fathering a child; he had a vasectomy soon after they married. But Vanessa doesn't tell Garrin, knowing there is no way back for them and believing him to be happy with

Amanda who is besotted with him.

Garrin focuses everything on the dream that replaced Vanessa, qualifying Derry for the Horse of the Year Show. On the day before he is due to compete, Isobel falls ill with meningitis. Stricken with guilt because he has cut Vanessa so completely from his life, Garrin forgoes his dream and returns to be with her and his daughter.

Forgiveness and revenge are the running themes and the story reaches its dramatic conclusion when Garrin and Vanessa wait at Isobel's bedside for news, each of them praying they won't lose another child. Their daughter's survival finally brings them together and they admit they have never stopped loving each other and never will.

Writing a synopsis for a short story

Is this even necessary? Once I would have said no, probably not. Most short stories can be sent off as they are to an editor, but, thanks to the digital age we are now in, times are changing.

Ebook publishers may well ask for a one sentence synopsis of your short story. And what good practice that is for an author. If you can sum up what your story is about in one sentence then it will stand you in very good stead for when you write a synopsis for your novel.

An example of a short story synopsis

At Her Time of Life

Dorothy finds out it's never to late to follow your dreams, especially where horses are concerned. (16 words)

Another example of a short story synopsis

A Souvenir from Skegness

Sarah doesn't believe in karma but when she gives up her holiday to help her sister, things certainly turn out well for her. (23 words)

As you can see, these are very short but they are long enough to tell an editor what your story is about. Enough of synopses. Let us move on to blurbs.

Writing a blurb for a novel

Traditionally, a blurb is what goes on the back cover of your novel and is used to sell it in a book shop or an online store. Prospective readers will scan the blurb to see if it catches their attention and if it does they may well buy it.

Some publishers/editors will write the blurb for you, but many of them won't and I think it's a useful skill for a writer to have. No one knows the book better than you, after all. Also, it's helpful to have a blurb handy when you are trying to sell your novel to an agent or publisher.

If you think of blurbs as selling tools, it might help you to write them more easily.

What should be in a blurb?

It should entice the reader to buy the book, as well as giving enough information to tell readers what sort of book they are buying, i.e. thriller, romance, historical. It should also introduce the main character/s and give an idea of the plot.

An example of a blurb for a novel

The following is the blurb for my novel, *Helter Skelter*.

Brought up on a seaside fairground, Vanessa knows all about what a rollercoaster ride life can be. Tragedy forces her to flee, but when she discovers that her husband, a property developer is cheating on her, she returns. But the fair has gone, the land, bought by her husband, is now covered in luxury flats. Going back can be painful but this is just the start of the Helter Skelter for Vanessa. While she feels her life is spiralling ever downwards, there are the strong arms of a passion from the past to catch her at the end.

Facts about this blurb

It has 98 words.
It introduces the main character by name.
It gives us a taste of the plot.
It gives us a taste of the setting
We know the book is probably a romance.

It uses strong words such as tragedy, cheating, luxury, passion. When you don't have many words at your disposal, they need to be chosen well.

Writing a blurb for your own novel, even if you have no intention of actually writing a novel at this moment, is an interesting exercise in itself as it teaches you how to focus on the bare bones of a story line. Who knows, you might be so taken with your blurb you want to write the book to find out what happens!

Go on, write a blurb. I dare you!

Writing a blurb for a short story

Once again, writing a blurb for a short story would not once have been necessary, but the digital age has changed things a bit. Short stories can now be sold online individually as well as in anthologies. Whether you are selling stories separately or in an anthology, a blurb is often needed as a selling tool.

If you think of blurbs in these terms, then they are quite easy to write. Imagine giving the reader a taster of what they are going to get.

Examples of short story blurbs

At her Time of Life

Dorothy had never imagined she'd learn to ride a horse at her time of life: she was a grandmother after all. But when she was housesitting for a week, the docile Candy Girl proved to be just too much of a temptation. (42 words)

A Souvenir from Skegness

When Sarah gave up her holiday plans to help out at her sister's ice cream stall in Skegness she imagined she'd also forgone the chance of any fun. But fun – and indeed romance – can turn up in the most unexpected places! (41 words)

Summary of differences

Synopses for short stories tend to be very short. Not much more than a sentence.

Novel synopses tend to be at least a page

Short story blurbs tend to be slightly shorter than novel blurbs, but there's not such a big difference generally. In both forms they are used as selling tools.

Chapter Seventeen
Feedback – Critique Services and Writing Classes

This chapter isn't strictly about making the leap between short story and novel writing, but because many new, and also more established, novelists think about using critique services for longer fiction, I thought it would be a good plan to say a little about them.

Should I use a professional critique service?

The short answer to this is, of course, that it's up to you. It probably depends on your motivation. Think about what you are trying to achieve. Do you want to get published? Do you want to improve your writing? Is it a bit of both?

No one can guarantee you publication, unless it's a publisher. And some publishers do have their own critique services. But even that cannot guarantee you publication. You are still going to need to write what they want. By the way, if a publisher does guarantee publication that's probably because it's selling its service, so do proceed with caution.

Wanting to improve your writing is a good reason to have a critique. Bear in mind you will need to act on what is said. What if you don't agree with it? What if you think the person critiquing has missed the point?

If you are going to spend a not inconsiderable amount

of money on a critique service then you really need to use one you respect and trust. It is pointless to consult a critique agency and then ignore what they say.

How do I find a good one?

If you want to get published then you need to find a critique service that a) is expert in your field, b) has current knowledge and c) has links with the industry, for example, they may be scouts for an agent too.

Look at what their website says. Do they have testimonials from previous clients who have gone on to get published in whatever field it is? Can you check them out? The credentials of the critique service are vital. Anyone can set one up but not all are successful or even very good.

Word of mouth is probably one of the best yardsticks there is. Do you know anyone who has used a critique service? You might not know them personally but perhaps you know them via an online group. Writing is quite a small world. Ask around. If you find someone ask him if he was happy with the service he got. Did he then go on to achieve publication? (If this is what you're looking for.) If not, why not?

How do they work?

Critique services usually charge a one-off fee for reading either an extract, for example, the first three chapters, or the whole of your manuscript. They will charge by the amount of words so obviously it will cost more for them to read the whole manuscript. When you approach one make sure you know exactly what is included. Are they going to give feedback and make suggestions about plot, characters and structure, or are they just going to offer a proof reading service? There is a world of difference between the two.

A good critique service will speak to you before critiquing your work so its staff know exactly what you wish to gain from your critique. Do check exactly what they are offering before you proceed.

Will they offer market advice? Is there a market for your manuscript, in terms of length, story etc.? This is vital if your aim is to get published. Will they look at any rewrites free of charge? Some may do this. Will they recommend your work to an agent if they think it's good enough? Personally, I think that a recommendation to an agent or publisher is worth its weight in gold.

Book doctors

Book doctors are similar to critique agencies, in that they critique manuscripts, but often they will work in a slightly different way. They will work with the writer on a one-to-one basis and they tend to charge by the hour rather than by the word. Rather than just focusing on one particular manuscript they will act as advisers in a more general way.

Critique services who are writers

Successful writers can make very good critics. After all, they know how to edit and appraise their own work so these skills are transferable – yes? Yes, but do proceed with caution. Not all successful writers are good critics. Writing and critiquing are different skills. Again, it is probably a wise move to ask for testimonials from writers they have helped.

How do I know if my novel is ready for a critique service?

One would hope, it goes without saying, that you should make sure your manuscript is as perfect as possible. I'm talking here about mistakes you know how to correct. It would be pretty pointless paying someone to tell you what you already know.

Sometimes, of course, especially when it comes to plot or character detail, you know something is wrong but you don't know how to correct it. This is where a critique service can really help. Or perhaps you think your manuscript is as good as it can be, but you still can't place it. It's possible a critique service could tell you why.

Costs of critique services

These vary enormously. You don't always get what you pay for. But with luck you shouldn't go too far wrong if you follow the advice given. Do check though, if you're paying by the hour, what proportion of your work is likely to be read.

Critiques are often offered as an additional perk in competitions, both short story and novel competitions. Obviously, the value of the critique depends on who is actually doing it, but if it's the judge – who might very well be offering a discounted rate – these can be a very good deal.

How to get the best value from a critique service

Critiques can be painful. However tactfully worded they are, and however much you trust the critic's opinion, it is your creation they are criticising – and you are probably going to be supersensitive about it. As writers we tend only to notice the bad things we're told. We skim over sentences like 'your characterisation is excellent', and home in on ones like 'your construction could do with some more work'.

We don't just *notice* the bad, we also tend to focus on it and rewrite the critic's true meaning. We tell our writer friends, "She said my characters were OK but my construction is hopeless. I'm never going to be a writer. I'm useless."

OK, I'm exaggerating a little, but we do tend to focus on the bad parts of a critique especially the first time we read it. It is very, very difficult to look at a critique of your own work with detachment. But this is exactly what you must do if you want to get the full value from it.

For this reason I strongly recommend that you don't act on your critique immediately. Read it, by all means, but then allow a cooling-off period (as you would do for your other edits) before you look at it again.

On a purely financial basis, some book doctors will offer their first hour free. Check this when you make your initial call.

While we're on the subject of getting the most out of a critique service, I spoke to Hilary Johnson of the Hilary Johnson Authors' Advisory Service, and this is what she has to say.

'The writers who most benefit from a critique service are those with a willingness to learn and an understanding that the purpose of criticism is not to diminish the author, but that it be *used* so that s/he, by following professional editorial advice, can, ultimately, produce a better book.'

Free critique services

I'm talking here mainly about groups of writers who get together to critique each other's work, either face to face or online. There can be immense value in these, especially if the critics really know what they are doing and are published in their field. Choose your group carefully. Again, if you can, try and get a personal recommendation to a group. Some of them are 'invitation only' and this can be a good thing.

Once you've found a group, here are some things to watch out for:

Drawbacks of free critique services

Follow my leader mentality

Sometimes the strongest member of a group will have an opinion and others will agree with them, even if they're wrong. It's sometimes more useful if individual members of a group, particularly an online group, give you individual feedback which is not based on what anyone else thinks. Then, if you do get repeat feedback, the chances are it's because you have room for improvement in that area, not because of any kind of 'follow my leader' mentality.

Inability to separate the writing from the subject

Sometimes a writer will criticise the writing, but actually it's the subject they don't like and the writing is fine. You can usually tell based on what they are saying.

Overview versus detail

Some groups will spend too much time on grammatical errors or tiny viewpoint slips or the use of a particular word and they will completely overlook the fact that actually the plot doesn't work anyway. You really need a group that can do both. It's relatively easy to focus on small details of a manuscript, but much harder to look at it as a whole.

Reading novels to groups section by section

While I think this can work, reading out small chunks of much larger manuscripts to groups can create problems. Pace is one of the classic examples. Pace needs to vary in novels; even if you're writing a speedy thriller you'll need to have sections where it slows down a little. Your group might not appreciate the slower pace in the context of faster-paced scenes around it, and vice versa. Sometimes it's tempting to 'up the tempo' of a piece of work just so that what you want to say fits in to the time section allowed by your group. This might not work when you are reading the novel as a whole. So do bear these things in mind.

Also, unless the group has heard every section of the novel, they might ask you to add information that you already have, for example, on the previous page.

It's much easier for critics, whoever they are, to judge a manuscript if they have the whole thing in front of them.

Writing classes

While I'm on the subject of feedback I should really mention writing classes and courses. Many creative writing classes offer students the opportunity to read out their work for feedback and constructive criticism. The advice I would give here is to find a tutor who knows your subject well. If you want to write novels and s/he has had or is having novels published then the advice should be useful. It also helps if tutors have expertise in your genre of writing. They might, for example, know all there is to know about the thriller market, but not so much about romance. But to be honest, most tutors who are published in one area are likely to have a broad-based knowledge of the industry and be in a position to help.

Courses

The above advice can also be applied to specialist residential courses. Choose a course with a good reputation, for example, the Arvon Foundation, and then pick your course not just on subject matter, but on what you know or can find out about the course leaders. What are their credentials? Do they have expertise in your area?

A degree in creative writing, by the way, does not make tutors experts on how to get published. Having a degree means they know the theory. An actual track record of publication means they are experienced in the real world, and the latter is far more helpful if getting published is your goal.

Retreats

This is a term used generally to describe places you can go to write, for example, cottages in idyllic locations, beaches, medieval castles (the latter if you're rich!). They are generally untutored, some are self-catering. Some even have services for writers such as cooks, or maids, so you can get on with the business of writing.

If you can't afford to head off to a castle or hire someone to do the domestic running around, booking a self-catering cottage for a weekend and splitting the cost and the cooking with a group of like-minded friends can be an excellent alternative.

A Friday night through to a Sunday evening works well, but if you can afford to go for longer, then that would probably be even better. I've been on a writer's retreat weekend and we split our time between actual writing, group exercises led by various members of the group, and reading out our work for constructive feedback.

Choose people you trust to comment on your work, as well as people whose company you enjoy.

Summer schools and conferences

These are more structured events run over weekends or sometimes over whole weeks. They are often themed, for example the Romantic Novelists Association runs an annual weekend conference, and I believe the Crime Writers Association also runs one. Dunford Novelists, held in January in Bournemouth is perfect for writers working on a specific novel.

If you'd rather go to a more general weekend conference, try Southern Writers, run each June in Chichester, or the one run by Ann and Gerry Hobbs in Fishguard, Pembrokeshire in February. Both are excellent.

Two week-long courses with excellent reputations are the Writers' Summer School at Swanwick, Derbyshire, in August – *swanwickwritersschool.co.uk* and the Writers' Holiday at Caerleon in July, also run by Ann and Gerry

Hobbs – *www.writersholiday.net.*

Literary festivals

There are dozens of literary festivals run across the country. New ones spring up each year so I'm not going to list them. But if you want to see if there is one near you it won't be difficult to find out via the internet. The events they arrange vary from library talks to competitions to tutored classes. They are worth checking out.

Summary of differences

Having your novel professionally critiqued will cost you a lot more than having a short story critiqued, for obvious reasons. But I think it's probably one of the most useful things a new novelist can do.

Bear in mind that if you're reading a small chunk of a novel to a group they can't always critique it in context.

For some reason many more people feel qualified to comment on short stories, or even critique them, when they don't have any relevant experience. This doesn't seem to happen so much with novels. But do be aware of this.

Chapter Eighteen
Competitions

Is it worth entering writing competitions?

Competitions are one of the ways in which you can get a track record, which never hurts. It's possible that you already have a writing track record. You may have had short stories published or won short story competitions. If this is the case then by all means tell your prospective agent or publisher in your covering letter.

But there are also many competitions for novels. Judges are usually looking for a first chapter or first few chapters, but occasionally they will be looking for a first page. So is it worth your while entering them?

Entering novel or partial novel competitions

If you have a brilliant first chapter then by all means enter it in a novel writing competition. If you are placed, then at the very least this is reassurance that you've written a good chapter.

Even better, see if you can find a competition organised by a publisher where a publishing contract is part of the prize. You will, of course, need to have written the whole novel for this. If not at the time you enter, then ultimately.

Do make sure you're not dealing with a self-publishing

organisation that is only running the competition as a marketing exercise. Check by asking other writers or looking online. Make sure the publisher is genuine. A good website to check out authenticity of both publishers and agents is Preditors and Editors – *pred-ed.com*.

Motivation for entering competitions

Mostly, I think we enter competitions for recognition. We want someone to say that what we've written is worthwhile. If you're looking for an endorsement of your work then make sure you enter a reputable competition. Don't forget that anyone can run writing competitions. The organisers don't need any qualifications or relevant experience, and writing competitions are seen by some as a good way to earn money.

How do I know if they are reputable?

If they are run by mainstream publishers, who don't ask authors to contribute to costs, then they usually are reputable. In fact, these can be an excellent way into publishing. Some competitions are run annually, in which case they will have a reputation, be it good or bad, so this is another good pointer.

This doesn't mean you shouldn't enter competitions that aren't run by a publisher, or that are new. But do tread carefully and bear in mind your motivation for entering. Some competitions, which don't result in a publishing deal, can also be worth entering. There are other useful prizes. For example, a critique by a well-known author is probably worth having.

Is it worth it?

Depending on what you want to gain, then yes, it probably is worth it. You have nothing to lose apart from the entry fee, and if you are highly placed in a reputable competition you may well catch the eye of an agent or publisher.

What if someone steals my idea?

I often get asked this question and, yes, there is always a possibility that this could happen. Would it actually be theft if they did? After all, there is no copyright on ideas. I think it's unlikely to happen, and even if someone did steal your idea they would still have to write the novel. Two or more people often have the same idea for a novel but that doesn't mean they will end up with the same novel.

However, just supposing you had a unique idea? This may be slightly different. I think if I felt I had a unique idea I wouldn't enter a competition. I'd simply get on with writing it and send it off to publishers.

Summary of differences

There aren't a lot of differences between entering short story competitions and entering novel writing competitions – except perhaps for the amount of work involved! Once again, though, I have noticed that people who are not qualified to judge fiction are far more likely to run a short story competition than they are a novel competition. So do check out the organiser's credentials.

Chapter Nineteen
Research

Research for short stories

It's important to get your facts right. It doesn't matter what length fiction you're writing. It's surprising how often I hear writers say, "Oh, it doesn't matter that much surely, it's only a story, after all. It's not real." Or words to that effect.

But actually it does matter. It's obvious when a writer hasn't researched properly and it jars. Think about it. Suppose, for example, you are a scuba diver and you are reading a novel where the main character is a diving instructor. How would you feel if he started to talk about something technical and you knew it was wrong? Or he used the wrong term for a piece of equipment. It would be annoying, wouldn't it? You would start to lose confidence in the story, possibly even in the writer. After all, he clearly doesn't know what he's talking about.

It sounds like a contradiction but it's important for fiction to have the 'believability' factor, although you might forgive the writer a small mistake in a short story.

Research for novels

It's even more important to get it right in a novel. Let's go back to your diving instructor. For one thing you will be writing about him with much more depth – pun intended – so he must come across as authentic. Therefore, if you're going to have a diving instructor hero, or heroine, make sure you know exactly what you're talking about. Or find someone who does.

OK, so you're a qualified diver, but you haven't dived for a while. You've got a good memory though, so you're OK – right? Wrong. Unless, of course, you're writing about the time period when you learnt to dive. Research must be current.

When I was writing *Helter Skelter* I had a main character who was a riding instructor. I'd had horses in the past, but I hadn't had a riding lesson for a few years, so I talked to someone who was currently teaching. Had it changed? Yes, it had changed quite a lot. In fact, some of the things they were teaching now were actually contrary to what I'd learnt. If I'd relied on my memory, I'd have been caught out completely.

Authenticity

Likewise, if you're writing a crime novel that involves police procedure – or even if part of your novel involves a character being questioned by the police, make sure you are accurate in what is said.

It's surprising how often you'll need to research something for a novel. Even quite common events, for example, paying a visit to hospital, rapidly change. Don't assume doctors wear white coats these days. Also, there aren't many hospitals you could visit which wouldn't have hand sterilisers at the entrance to wards. When were these introduced? It's adding authentic details like this which will bring your scene to life and make it believable to readers.

I think you'll agree that nothing is more off-putting than reading a scene, where the author clearly has no idea of his facts.

Timings

One of the types of research I find myself doing a lot involves what time things happen. For example, I might want to know what plants are in bloom in April, or when it's the best time to plant tomatoes, or what time it gets dark in October.

There is a great deal of information to be found on the internet, but do check more than one source. For general facts and figures there are some very helpful websites too. *www.timeanddate.com* shows sunrise and sunset (which is not necessarily quite the same thing as when it gets dark – but is close).

www.timeanddate.com/worldclock. This one – as the name suggests – tells you what time it is anywhere in the world.

If, like me, you have a hopeless memory, you can do a lot worse than keep your own personal record of facts and figures that you think might come in useful.

Some time ago I created a document in which I listed, among other things, what plants/crops/flowers, etc. were out in any given month, what time it got light and dark in Dorset, and what birds/wildlife were around. My list serves me well. Every time I need to add some authentic detail, usually to enhance my settings, I consult my list. I also find it's quite useful to make a note of when things are early or late, for example, an early snow, or late bluebells.

A daily diary is also an excellent memory jogger.

Journey times

While we're on the subject of timings I should mention journey times. Do make sure you get these right, particularly if you're not familiar with the area. Also, how is your character travelling? If it's by public transport, then make sure it exists in the area you're talking about. Otherwise an over-zealous local may well be tempted to write to your publisher and inform them you got it wrong!

Plotting

Research can help with plotting. Several times I have come across facts I haven't previously known about and have found them useful for my plot. Research adds authentic detail, although don't fall into the trap of shoe-horning large chunks of your research into your novel, simply because you have done it. This can get quite tedious for the reader.

Characters – real or fictional

Although I'm not suggesting you base your characters on real people, we do tend to get our ideas from life – so real characteristics creep into our fictional people.

Two writers I know, who write historical fiction, actually do use characters from their own family tree. This isn't something I've done yet but I think it's a fascinating exercise. It's surprising what you can find out about your ancestors by looking at old records, for example, what age they got married, how many children they had, if they were divorced, where they lived, what they did, if they had any money problems or convictions.

All these things can give you an outline of what the

real person was like and you can make up the rest – you're a writer. Well, you can if you are writing a fictional account. What could be more fun than writing a fictional account of what happened in the past? Half the storyline is there already, you just need to fill in the gaps.

If you want to write a novel but are stuck for a plot then you could do a lot worse than researching your own family tree. Who was Great-great-uncle Albert on your father's side, who gave up his inheritance to run off with a woman in service? Or how about Mary, a distant relative of your grandmother's, who was once imprisoned for being involved with the Emmeline Pankhurst and the suffragette movement? You don't have to write about these people in their time, you could pluck them out of history and bring them into the 21st century. Let them live their lives again in contemporary times.

Using the internet

As I've already mentioned the internet is a fantastic research tool, but it's worth remembering that things you read on the internet are not necessarily correct. In the days before computers when writers had to go to libraries to do research – however did we manage? – We were told to check three separate sources when it came to facts. It's a good idea to follow this advice when it comes to the internet too. If anything, it is less reliable than reference books you might find in libraries because reference books have gone through a checking and editing process. Most websites have not. In fact, sometimes incorrect information is perpetuated by others who have assumed it to be true.

Another of the things I find the internet invaluable for, when it comes to both short stories and novels, is its surfeit of real life stories/blogs. If you want to know, for example, how it feels to be a soldier in Afghanistan, or a midwife in Somalia there is almost certainly someone out there who knows and has written about it.

Likewise, if you want to know how it feels to have: lost a baby; had cancer; got married to sixteen people; learned to fly a plane, etc., there is probably a blog on it.

Blogs are brilliant research tools for writers. They tell you how it feels. This is something you can't get from reference books. Once, you would have had to track people down and talk to them to find out. The internet makes it easy. They don't even have to know you are reading their blogs.

Talking to people about their experiences directly is still a good research tool, by the way. Do that, too, if you can.

Research is never wasted. One of the things I love about writing is that it's a constant learning experience. How many other jobs are there where you are constantly finding out new things?

Summary of differences

There are not a lot of differences between short and long fiction when it comes to research. Both forms need authenticity.

The only one I can think of is that while you might get away with skimming on research for a short story because the depth required is not so great, lack of research will show up in a novel. If you don't know what you're talking about your reader will catch you out.

Chapter Twenty
Setting

Setting in the short story

As I've already mentioned, setting in a short story will tend to be brushstroked in. It's important to have a feel of a place in the background, otherwise your characters will be moving through a vacuum, the story has to take place somewhere, but the setting isn't quite as important as it is in a novel.

Introducing setting in a short story – example

Here's an example of setting being introduced in a short story: This is a very short story – around 1200 words.

From *Picture Perfect* (published in *My Weekly*)

As Val walked through the foyer towards the bar at the front of the hotel she could see she wasn't the first to arrive. Jenny and Thelma were already at their usual table. Bordered by pot plants and with an outlook straight across the sea, it was the best table in the bar.

We know we're in a bar by the sea – that is all we need to know. We don't know the name of the bar or which beach. We don't need to know this. We then move away from the setting and into the story.

Here's a bit more setting from later on in the story.

It wasn't that she didn't like babies, Val mused, as she gazed out across the sea which was in full blue sparkle today and already dotted with surfers. She could hear children's shrieks and the swoosh of the sea; the sounds of the coast creeping through the open windows with the ozone scented air.

Once more, the setting is really just a backing track to Val's thoughts. The beach is, in fact, quite relevant to the story because Val and her husband spend a lot of time on their boat but it isn't intrusive.

Here's a touch more setting: Really it's only the last line that is setting.

The next time she did get the chance to catch up with them it was late August and they'd had to make their meeting a bit earlier in order to be sure of getting a table. The place was full of sunshine and families.

After this there's only one further mention of setting. See below.

As she sat there with her two closest friends in the sunlight streaming through from the beach, she knew this was one time when she didn't mind feeling left out at all.

So during this entire story of 1200 words, we only have 150 words or so of setting. This is what I mean by brushstroking in the setting. It's there, but it's subtle.

Setting in the novel

So, to continue with my painting analogy, if you brushstroke setting into a short story, do you dollop it in great lumps into a novel? No, of course not. Actually, I think you can still brushstroke it in, perhaps build it up in layers as you would in a fine oil painting, but you definitely need more depth.

In *Picture Perfect* we don't know where in the country the story is taking place, we only know it's on the coast. That's deliberate. I wanted it to be a universal story. I wanted every woman who read it to picture a different beach. I quite often do that with stories and it works, but it's a lot harder to get away with it in a novel. And I'm not so sure you should do it there. Readers need more depth, more placement, more identification. It is rather nice to read about a place you know well. It can add an extra dimension to a novel.

It's nice to read about a real place in a short story too, but my point here is that you do not have to set a short story in a real place, whereas in a novel you do need to be more specific.

Should I use a real place to set my novel?

I think it's a good idea to use a real place as a novel setting. You don't have to be totally specific, although you can be if you wish. Why not use London or Manchester or Dundee? If you know and love these places then you can bring them alive. You can have your characters strolling down real streets, or in the case of cities, going into real high street shops and museums. These details will ground your story and bring your characters to life. Do, of course, be careful about libel. It would not, for example, be advisable to have your characters going into a real restaurant and then having a disastrous meal. Naturally, this would be likely to upset the proprietors!

If you need your characters to have a disastrous meal in a real city then make up the name of the restaurant and, if necessary, the street. Do check that you have actually made it up too and that you are not dredging it out of your subconscious. It might be advisable to check there is no restaurant of that name nearby too! Something I do quite often is to invent fictitious names for pubs and places.

If you're setting your novel somewhere reasonably small, like a village, then it's a good plan to make up the village name. By all means use a real county if you like. *Passing Shadows* was set in Wiltshire. Maggie, the main character, lives in a village near Salisbury called Arleston. There is no such place as Arleston. I made it up for the purposes of the novel.

For *Helter Skelter*, which was set in the Purbecks, I did something slightly different. I used some of Thomas Hardy's fictitious place names, but in order to avoid any kind of copyright issues I changed the spelling slightly. So, for example, Knollsea, which was Thomas Hardy's fictitious name for Swanage, became Knollsey in my novel. This was quite good fun. I knew that readers of Hardy (if any of them read *Helter Skelter*) would recognise the names and, with luck, smile.

Changing names

Another possibility is to use a real place, verbatim, and change all the names. For example, if your novel was set in the town of Milford on Sea you could call it Shelford on Sea. You would also make up street names and names for other landmarks. The advantage of doing this is that you don't have to invent a whole new place – you're simply changing names, so the logistics will be correct. Neither will you invite any libel actions from locals!

Generally a good tip would be to use real place names for big places, i.e. counties, and make them up for smaller towns or villages. This way, your reader can get a good picture of your location without you having to be too specific.

So you might have a fictitious village in a real county, or on the outskirts of a real town. Or you might have a fictitious road or business park in a real town. This would also be fine.

Creating maps

This might sound a little excessive, but I'm not talking about creating maps on a grand scale (although you can if you want to!). I find it quite helpful when I'm writing something longer to have at least a floor plan of anywhere my characters are going to visit more than once. It's no good having them turn left to the kitchen, which is at the front of the house, on page 1 and then right to the kitchen at the back of the house on page 144. You may have completely forgotten the exact placement of the kitchen by page 144.

This is unlikely, I know, but it's possible. If you're the sort of person who can hold a map in your head (you can probably find your way around strange towns too) then you won't need any visual aid. If, like me, you're not, then you may find it very useful. *Passing Shadows* was set in an animal sanctuary, complete with outbuildings, kennels, fields, etc., and I had a floor plan of the whole place.

If you don't want to invent a floor plan then you could use the floor plans of real houses. Estate agent websites are a good source of floor plans.

Introducing setting in a novel – example

Here is an example of introducing setting in a novel. Maggie and Finn are in Skegness and the section is in Maggie's viewpoint.

Extract from *Passing Shadows*

At the end of the street, the tarmac gave way to a track and then to sand and there was a new, salt freshness in the air. Finn gestured her down some steps ahead of him and she realised they were on the beach. The tide was out, leaving a great expanse of sand stretching down towards the dark sea. A moon path lay across the water, a strip of silver glitter on a piece of black paper. Like a child's drawing, Maggie thought, reminded of Ben and his pictures, as she followed Finn towards the hard sand at the water's edge.

We are shown the beach via Maggie's viewpoint, as opposed to just seeing it through the narrative. She likens the moon path across the water to a child's drawing. This is very pertinent to the story because both Finn and his son, Ben, are artists. For me, setting should always be coloured by a character's viewpoint. Note, the character's viewpoint, not the author's.

Here is another section, also in Maggie's viewpoint.
She strolled along the quiet roads past untidy hedges that spilled out like overgrown mops of hair, revelling in the

peace and enjoying the clear honey-coloured light that preceded sunset.

Ten minutes later, she was letting herself through the lichen-covered gate of the churchyard, aware of the small wooden thud as it swung shut behind her. She walked slowly along the mossy, cobbled path between the graves. It seemed rude to run through a cemetery, disrespectful somehow, and however much she longed for this visit to be over she didn't want to offend anyone. These people, whose headstones rose higgledy-piggledy from the ground on either side of her, seemed almost like friends: their names were so familiar, and she'd often wondered about their lives.

Again, the setting is given, but sparsely, via Maggie's viewpoint. The untidy hedges and the light are depicted without extensive detail. We know the gate is wood and not large because of the small wooden thud – again no need to describe in detail. We can guess the cemetery is old because of the moss and the lichen and the higgledy-piggledy headstones. Then we are given a sense of Maggie's character. *'It seemed rude to run through a cemetery, disrespectful somehow...'*

In this extract we are revealing not just the setting, but her character, which brings me on to another point. Setting, character and plot need to be threaded together in contemporary fiction, which I hope is illustrated by the above examples.

Summary of differences

It's not necessary to tell the reader where your characters are, specifically, in a short story. In fact, sometimes it can be an advantage not to. If you are setting your story on a beach or by a river, the reader can fill in the details. Each reader will have a different beach, a different river and this is rather nice. A short story setting can be universal.

Not so in a novel. Generally speaking, settings need to be clearly defined. Which country? Which part of the country? Even which town? All of these things must be clear to the author and to the reader.

Maps and floor plans are very useful when you're writing longer fiction, particularly if you've invented a setting. They're not so essential for short stories for obvious reasons.

In both short stories and novels, setting should be shown through your characters' viewpoints. It should be threaded in through the narrative. The techniques are similar, that is: brushstrokes as opposed to great swathes of description, but in novels you can built setting, layer upon layer.

Chapter Twenty-one
Finding an Agent or Publisher

Finding an agent or publisher to sell your work has traditionally been part of writing a novel. And this is something you don't need to do if you write short stories. Well, you don't need an agent to sell your short stories, but you will of course need a publisher. More of that later. I'll assume you are writing a novel for now. And I'll assume you would like to find an agent or publisher.

Times are actually changing. There are other alternatives now, but more of that later in this chapter, too.

Which is best – agent or publisher?

In my experience the answer to the agent or publisher question depends very much on what you are writing and what you want to achieve. If you have set your heart on breaking into the novel market and you are looking for a big mainstream publisher who you hope is going to offer you a six-figure deal – and let's face it, who isn't? – then you probably do need an agent. Many of the big publishing houses won't even look at unsolicited manuscripts, that is, ones that have not been submitted via ʼt.

of them will look at unsolicited manuscripts, Check out their websites, or the Writer's

Handbook or Writers and Artists' Year guidance. One or two even have their own eh systems (dubbed an electronic slush pile) prospective authors can upload their books.

Harper Collins has an online system called *authonomy.com* which invites authors to upload the first 10,000 words of their novels which will then receive feedback from the online community. There is a possibility that a good novel will be spotted and taken on.

However, to go back to my original question, which is best, agent or publisher, I would be tempted to try and find an agent first. From a purely practical basis, if you submit your manuscript to several publishers and they turn it down, and then you subsequently find an agent there seems little point in your agent resubmitting a novel that has already been rejected.

What will a good agent do for me?

A good agent will negotiate the aforementioned six-figure deal, should you get one! They are, joking aside, in a much better position to get you a deal in the first place because it's their job to know what's going on in the publishing world. It's their job to know who is looking for what type of book at any given moment.

A good agent will also give you advice and guidance on your writing. Many have strong editorial backgrounds. Nice ones also support and mentor you through the inevitable rejections. Just because an agent has a lot of faith in your novel, and she will have if she takes you on, it doesn't mean she will be able to sell it. Publishing is a very fickle business.

Can I approach a publisher direct?

Yes you can, providing its submission guidelines permit it. Also, many smaller publishers prefer to deal with writers direct. There are advantages in dealing with a smaller publisher. OK, so you might not get a big advance, or any advance at all, these days, but that doesn't mean you can't make any money. Some novels, which started off with small publishers subsequently made it on to the best-seller lists. Stieg Larsson's trilogy, published by Quercus, springs to mind. Larsson's three novels, *The Girl with the Dragon Tattoo, The Girl Who Played with Fire* and *The Girl Who Kicked the Hornet's Nest* are all bestsellers.

Some novels which started off as self-published novels have also made it on to the best-seller lists. Beatrix Potter's *A Tale of Peter Rabbit* was originally self-published after she received rejections from the six publishers she approached. Undeterred, she published 250 copies herself. The rest, as they say, is history.

Smaller publishers versus bigger publishers

Smaller publishers can't always offer big advances, but there are other advantages of working with them. Often you will have more say in things like covers and other editorial issues, for example, the blurb on the back of the book.

Both big and small publishers will expect you to do a lot of the publicity work yourself, these days, which is no bad thing as finding out what sells books is a useful skill for writers to have, particularly when they come to write their next book.

Direct publishing (electronically)

Thanks to the digital age, these days there is another option. You don't need anyone's help to publish your book electronically. You can do it yourself. Amazon has a system where writers can upload their work to be sold in its Kindle format.

There are also other publishers and booksellers who will work in partnership with writers direct. They provide websites where writers can upload their novels, or in some cases short stories, to be sold direct to the public. The writers will generally need to provide their own covers and ISBN numbers and then profits are split between author and bookseller.

If you do choose this route I would strongly advise you to employ a proof reader before uploading your manuscript. It's very hard to proofread your own work with 100 per cent accuracy.

Self-publishing

You can, of course, also self-publish your book in print if you wish. There are many self-publishing packages available. If you decide to self-publish your book then do think carefully how you are going to distribute it and sell it. This is probably the hardest part of self-publishing. And it's important to have some sort of marketing action plan in mind.

Short stories and epublishing

I want to mention short stories briefly here because I think that the rise of digital publishing is very good news for short-story writers. Just as writers can upload their own novel and sell it via various publishers' and book sellers' websites, so they can upload short stories and do the same. Being able to sell direct to readers can only improve things for writers (if not for agents and publishers).

I think this will happen more and more. Finding a publisher for a collection of short stories has always been difficult. Traditionally, they don't sell well unless the author is already famous. Therefore, publishers haven't been keen to buy them.

But estories can, of course, be downloaded individually, which can be a more attractive option for buyers, and I foresee this being a big market in the future.

The submission package

If you are taking the traditional route and approaching publishers or agents, then they will usually require a submission package of three chapters and a synopsis. Whether you send this electronically or on paper will depend on their individual guidelines.

Most publishers require between one and three chapters of your novel – and they generally mean the first three chapters, not random chapters, a synopsis, and a biography. Some will require a blurb as well. For details of writing a synopsis and blurb, please see Chapter Sixteen.

Writing a biography

In addition, you might also need to provide a brief biography. The function of a biography is to show you have a track record. This might be in the form of writing experience, for example, you've had several short stories published in magazines, or it might be related to the subject of your book. You need to include anything you think is relevant. For example, if your book is about recovering from alcoholism and you are a recovering alcoholic then say so. Likewise, if you have years of experience working as a proof reader or you are a marketing expert, this may also be relevant.

Ultimately, a biography is only background information to the actual work you are sending. It won't help you get an offer, necessarily; although it might convince a publisher you have the requisite experience.

A biography should be written in third person. This is the biography I wrote for this particular book. Bear in mind that this is a biography for a non-fiction book.

Biography

Della Galton has been selling short stories for over 20 years. She sells between 80 and 90 short stories a year to markets in the UK and abroad.

Her first two novels, PASSING SHADOWS and HELTER SKELTER were published by Accent Press.

She is also a commissioning editor for a publisher, a popular speaker at writers' conferences across the UK and the agony aunt for Writers' Forum Magazine.

Biographies, like everything else you send to publishers, should be targeted to show your experience for that particular book.

It's not so common to be asked for a biography when you submit a short story, but, if you were asked, it would probably be much shorter. A couple of sentences are probably enough. I could just use the first two sentences of the biography shown above.

Incidentally, if you do self-publish a novel and it doesn't sell very well, it is wise not to mention this at all in your biography to a mainstream publisher. It won't help your case and might, in fact, even put them off.

Ebooks and print on demand

I've already mentioned ebooks, but before we leave the subject I'd like to add a couple of other things. If you do end up getting a contract with a publisher, they will also produce your book in ebook format and possibly various other formats, including audio. Details of your share of these royalties will come under the royalties sections of your contract.

If you don't have an agent to check your contracts for you, then do pay close attention to what is being offered. Ebooks may very possibly be outselling print books soon and these rights are vital to a writer. Make sure you negotiate them in your favour. If you don't have an agent it is worth becoming a member of The Society of Authors, as, at the time of writing, their members are entitled to a free contract check.

Print on demand simply means that your publisher will print books as and when they are ordered. This saves publishers from ending up with huge piles of books they cannot sell, but it does tend to put the onus on the writer to find the buyers for their own books.

Summary of differences

Traditionally, you needed to approach an agent or publisher to sell your novel. (Although as we have seen this is changing).

You can approach an epublisher or magazine direct to sell short stories, presuming they want short stories.

The industry is changing very quickly because of electronic publishing. It is now possible for a new writer to sell both short stories and novels directly to the reader.

Chapter Twenty-two
Marketing and Publicity

One of the nice things about having a book published is that you can have a book launch. You may have had short stories published in a magazine or small press, or online but none of these mediums lend themselves to launches, unfortunately. Magazines are fleeting, they're on the shelves for a week or two and then they are gone. I remember how excited I was when my first book was published. Planning a book launch is pure pleasure, as well as being a commercial exercise to sell books, of course.

How do I organise a book launch?

It's simple. You find a venue, usually a book shop, although it certainly doesn't have to be a book shop. And then you invite everyone you know. Here's a list of tips from my own experience:

Timing

The most important factor is, naturally, having books to sell. For this reason, it's not advisable to have a book launch too close to publication date, just in case there are any hold-ups or delays. Nothing is more depressing than planning a launch and then discovering your book won't now be published until the week after. I know one or two people who this has happened to – and while they did manage to get people to order their book at the launch, which still went ahead, it's not quite the same as signing copies on the day! Speak to your publisher if you have one. Find out exactly when the books are going to be available to you.

I usually time my launches for around three weeks after publication date and then I keep a close eye on proceedings.

Venue

As I've mentioned, traditionally this is a book shop, but it doesn't have to be. Much will depend on how many people you are going to invite. I've also used pubs and halls, which are quite good, particularly if people are travelling and you want to provide refreshments. You may also want to consider using your local library or community centre.

Publishers will often arrange signings for you at chains like WH Smith, and if you are organising your own you can do the same. Or you might prefer to approach your local book shop. They will usually be glad of the opportunity to sell books. Your publisher will usually provide posters, if asked. Again, if you are self-publishing, you can design your own posters.

Advertising your launch

You may wish to extend your launch invitation to members of the public. If you are holding your launch in a bookshop, ask them if they'll display posters or leaflets on

171

the counter for you. You could also send press releases to local magazines or newspapers. At my last launch I happened to be doing a radio interview and I mentioned my launch on air. I was pleasantly surprised when about 6 people I didn't know turned up for the event, having heard me talking on the radio. Radio interviews obviously work.

Refreshments

You will probably want to provide refreshments for your guests. Drinks and nibbles are good. Obviously you won't want anything too major (or messy) in a book shop, but wine and soft drinks are a nice touch. You might want to separate the refreshments from the actual book launch. Many writers sign books first in a book shop or other venue and then hire a hall close by, where refreshments are served afterwards. You might even want to hold a party at your home for guests to attend afterwards.

Invites/press releases

I've found it useful to send out invitations by post and I ask people to RSVP so I know the numbers I'm catering for. You could, if you prefer, do this by email, or even by phone, depending on your circumstances.

If you do send out press releases, keep them brief. You'll need to state the title of the book, the author, the time and date of the launch and a couple of sentences about your book to entice people to come along.

Giving talks

If you are adept at giving talks, and if you aren't, it might be a good plan to learn the skills, then this is a good way to publicise your books. Offer your services (for free if necessary) to local groups. Lots of groups are interested in writers and getting published. People like to hear about people and their experiences.

I have given talks at writing groups, WI groups, libraries, people's houses, hotels (as an after dinner speaker). I was even an after-dinner speaker at a Jewish convention once – they threw in a free tour of the synagogue, which was most interesting.

Make sure you can take your books along to sell after the talk, and emphasise what good birthday and Christmas presents signed copies make!

Doing signings

You don't need to confine signings to your launch. You could arrange signings at book shops after publication date if you want to. You might also want to run workshops for writers and take books along to those too.

Websites, blogs and other marketing via the internet

Do you blog or tweet or have a Facebook account? At the very least you should, as a writer, have your own website. You can say a bit about your book on your website and can advertise signed copies also. Blogging, that is, using an online diary, where you can talk about your book, is a good marketing tool. Don't just use your blog as a self promoting tool, as people are likely to get tired of that – use it as a place to give out information. Ditto if you use Twitter.

Other types of publicity

Magazine publicity

If you have short stories published regularly in magazines or small presses or online, then ask the magazines, etc. if they would mention your novel title and where to buy it beneath your byline at the bottom of the story.

You could take out your own adverts in magazines. This probably works better if you are targeting a specific audience. For example, if you have written a novel set in a particular town, you could advertise it locally, or if you have written a novel set in an animal sanctuary, you could ask other animal sanctuaries if they will sell copies of your novel.

There are other, perhaps quirkier, ways of selling books, particularly if your book is specialist interest. One of my books, *The Dog with Nine Lives*, which is actually non-fiction, focuses on a dog I rescued from Greece. This story is close to my heart and so as well as selling it through the traditional routes, like bookshops, I also sell it through a 'dog rescue organisation' (it is advertised on their website. DAWGdogs.net) and I donate the profits to their organisation.

Selling your book on behalf of your favourite charity is a great way to raise money for them and is very satisfying.

Competition publicity

You might even want to run a competition to promote your novel. Perhaps it could be a mini writing competition. Local magazines might well be interested in doing this, especially if you are going to judge the competition and offer signed copies of your novel as prizes. Ask them.

General publicity

I was once told by another writer never to go anywhere without a few copies of my books in my car. It's amazing how often the opportunity to sell a book comes up. My husband, Tony, is particularly brilliant at selling my books. He recently sold one to a guest at a wedding we were at. He has no shame at all.

Summary of differences

Generally speaking, short stories don't need to be launched. Although, I suppose you could have a party to celebrate publication of your next short story – why not? Any excuse for a party, I say!

Chapter Twenty-three
How to Deal with Rejection

Coping with rejection

One of the things that stopped me from having any serious attempts at writing a novel was the fear of rejection. It was bad enough when I sent a short story of a thousand or two thousand words to a publisher and they decided they didn't want it. I wasn't sure if I could bear to write seventy or eighty thousand words and have that rejected too.

Maybe you feel the same. What can be done about it? Well, the short answer is, absolutely nothing. Unless of course you want to give up the whole idea of writing a novel because then you won't have to face the possibility of rejection. But I doubt you'd have read this far if you were a "giving up" sort of person, would you!

If you are going to write a novel and send it off to an agent or publisher, there is a high chance you will collect some rejection slips. In fact, I don't know any writer who has never had a rejection slip, although there may well be such a lucky person out there. And I say lucky because there is definitely an element of luck in being published.

Reasons for rejection

These are exactly the same for short stories as they are for novels: they are things like subject matter; poor quality; inaccurate targeting; bad timing.

But really there is only one reason for novel rejections. The publisher (or agent) doesn't think they can sell the novel at that time. It might, however, be a best seller a couple of years later! In fact, I have known novelists who have been rejected countless times and then a few years later had the very same novel accepted by one of the original publishers.

The main point to observe here is that the writer obviously didn't give up!

Lessening the pain

Perhaps fear of rejection is the reason that some writers self-publish. In the same way that some writers start up their own magazines in order to publish their short stories, some prospective novelists go straight into self-publishing. And if this is the route you want to take, then good luck to you.

But if you don't want to go straight down the self-publishing route then there are things you can do to help minimise the pain of rejection. There are also things you can do to help minimise the chances of it happening in the first place. Prevention is better than cure, they say, so let's start with the preventative measures.

Preventative measures

Make sure your manuscript is as perfect as you can make it. By that, I mean, make sure it is your final draft and not your "almost final" draft. One of the biggest mistakes authors make is to send out their work too soon. This is a shame, especially when you consider how long it takes to write something. If you have slaved over a story for a year or more, an extra week or two isn't going to make any difference, but it could make all the difference to your chances of acceptance, or at least to your chances of actually getting your submission read.

It's especially important to check your first page. I've been working as an editor for a publisher for two years, so I'm going to briefly slip my editor's hat on here and tell you how it is from the other side of the fence.

I've had the chance to read numerous submissions and it's astonishing how many of them have mistakes on the first page.

This screams "Amateur". One mistake is possibly forgivable, two is sloppy, three is annoying and I would probably stop reading and move on to the next submission. (If I was in a bad mood, I might do it after two mistakes.)

The manuscript might be absolutely brilliant (I'm guessing it isn't), but I won't know because I haven't pursued it. The publisher I work for receives so many submissions I simply don't have time to read work that appears to be shoddy. We already receive more novels than we can publish that are beautifully written and presented. Why would we want to waste our time reading poorly presented submissions?

Never forget this. It's a bit like going for an interview, having done a whole pile of research for the job, and then turning up with uncombed hair and a black mark on your suit. It simply isn't professional. First impressions aren't everything, but they are *very* important.

Also, do make sure you've sent your manuscript to the right place. All publishers have guidelines which state what they do and do NOT want to receive. Read them and adhere to them. If your publisher says they are looking for novels between 70,000 and 90,000 words they probably do mean it. They are unlikely to consider a 45,000 word manuscript, however brilliant it is.

Likewise, if they say they don't want sci fi or children's fiction, they probably mean that too. They won't be swayed by your letter telling them that you can make them rich. Incidentally, I didn't think writers actually wrote letters like this before I became an editor, but they do!

While it's nice to see a writer is confident, it's slightly disconcerting when they begin their introductory email with the words "I am writing to give you the opportunity to make a lot of money." I am not making this up by the way; we've had letters that really do start like this! Perhaps they work in sales.

Anyway, my point is to let your writing speak for itself. All you need to say in any covering letter or email is what you are submitting plus anything else the publisher's guidelines have asked for. For example, if they ask for a brief biography, blurb and three chapters, then this is what you should send.

It's also quite nice when writers address the editor by name, as opposed to saying just, "hi", or "hey" or "yo guys!" Finding out an editor's name doesn't take much effort as it's usually stated on the guidelines.

Incidentally, while I'm on the subject of names, I've occasionally had writers address me as hey or hi when we've actually been in correspondence for a while and I'm clearly signing my name on the bottom of my email and addressing them by theirs, which I was taught was polite. This is even more disconcerting.

Chasing up manuscripts

Waiting to hear your manuscript's fate is very frustrating.

I know this as a writer, but I also know, having been a professional writer for twenty-five years that one of the attributes you need to have by the bucket-load is patience.

Because I have seen things from both side of the fence so to speak, I try not to keep writers waiting, but there is always going to be a delay. It takes time to read submissions and time to decide whether they are suitable. Try to be patient. Emailing after a week or two, or even a month, is not very patient.

As a writer I would expect to wait at least a couple of months before I heard about a longer submission. I would probably wait three months before chasing. If you're in doubt about how long to wait, then check the agent or publisher's guidelines, as they will often tell you how long they expect to be before giving you a response.

I regularly wait five or six months to hear about a short story's fate, which also helps to put it in perspective. In fact, on this basis, most agents/publishers respond very quickly.

Sometimes, chasing up a manuscript can result in a rejection. This happens because overworked editors, who know they are behind with their reading, may simply grab the opportunity to reduce their reading pile. Put yourself in their place – imagine a writer is asking for a manuscript they haven't yet read, what are they likely to think? Perhaps, "Ha ha, the writer obviously wants his manuscript back swiftly so I'll send it back to him, and it'll be one less for me to read." This is, after all, human nature. For this reason I don't chase manuscripts unless I really *do* want them back.

Multi-submissions

Should you send your novel out to more than one

agent/publisher at a time? This is a difficult question with no right answer. Some agents say they don't mind, some say they hate it. It isn't difficult to see why they might hate it. Let's assume they've just spent two or three hours of their valuable time reading it and are really excited about it – it's the best thing that's landed on their desk since Harry Potter. Then they get a letter or an email from you saying you'd like to withdraw the submission because you have found representation elsewhere.

What a frustrating waste of time that would be!

Now, let's stand on the other side of the fence for a moment. If you send out your novel to ten agents, one at a time, and they all take two months to reject it, then you will have wasted an inordinate amount of time.

I think that you have to decide for yourself on this one. This is my opinion from both sides of the fence:

As an editor, I am perfectly happy to receive simultaneous submissions of proposals (three chapters and a synopsis) as long as the writer makes it clear that's what s/he is doing, that is, s/he tells me (politely) in the covering letter. I would not be so keen if we'd got a stage further than that and I'd asked to see and read the whole novel and then it was snatched away, as obviously I'd have invested a lot more time in it.

As a writer I would also send out simultaneous submissions, but only in certain circumstances. If I'd developed any kind of relationship with an agent or publisher, for example, I'd met them at a writers' conference or been recommended by another writer or mutual friend then I'd give them the manuscript solely and I'd make that clear in my covering letter.

If I didn't know the agent, let's suppose I was trying to break into a different market, non-fiction instead of fiction, and maybe I'd found them in the course of some research, then I would have no qualms about sending a multi submission.

This is purely my take on it. You might feel differently.

Rewrites

When it comes to novels don't rewrite unless an agent or editor asks you to do so. Well, obviously you can rewrite, but don't send the rewrite back to them unless they have asked to see it. Sometimes they might say something like, "This wasn't quite right for me, but I'd be happy to see your next novel."

This is frustrating I know, especially as you probably haven't written your next novel. But you're going to, aren't you? So it's a very good plan to keep a note of that agent or editor's name for future reference.

Sometimes editors or agents may ask for a rewrite on work that they've seen. Usually they will have seen the whole manuscript if they are asking for a rewrite. If they do this it means that they like your work a lot and you are very close to a standard they think is publishable. They wouldn't ask you unless they were confident of this.

If you do find yourself in this situation, then it's a good idea to do the rewrite as quickly as possible. Just because someone is excited by your work now doesn't mean he will be equally excited by it in a year or two's time.

On a similar note, if having sent your three chapters and a synopsis, someone asks to see the rest, do send it as quickly as possible. I know that not all writers finish their novels before sending in the first three chapters, and then it's a frantic rush to write the rest if an agent asks to see it. This does seem to work for some – but I wouldn't personally recommend it, particularly if you haven't written a novel before. How do you know you are going to be able to finish it for a start? Also, if you look at this from an agent's perspective, aren't you being a teeny bit selfish?

They can't sell three chapters. They can only sell the whole novel. And if you haven't yet written it they may well have wasted their time reading the three chapters. This was another consideration that hadn't occurred to me before I was given a job as an editor and could see things from the other side of the fence.

Another good reason for finishing the entire novel before you send it anywhere is this: if an agent or editor doesn't like your first three chapters you might feel so disheartened that you decide not to finish it at all. This would be awful because it might be a perfectly fine three chapters, but it just wasn't suitable for that particular agent at that particular time. No, let's move on to coping with rejections.

Short story rejections

If you've read my book *How to Write and Sell Short Stories* you'll know that my advice to short story writers is to send out lots of stories. If you have one short story out and it comes back – all hope is lost. It you have two pieces out and one comes back, 50% of hope is lost. If you have 20 or 30 pieces out and one comes back, then – *So what?* The more pieces you have out, the more those individual rejections are diluted. Make sure that you have enough work circulating to generate the *so what?* factor.

Novel rejections

Unfortunately, this isn't quite as easy to do with novels.

Unless you are planning to write 20 or 30 novels before you send any out, which would be silly, wouldn't it! Although I suppose it's an option if you start writing young! I am joking, of course.

Fortunately, there are things you can do which will lessen the pain of rejection. One of them is to get on immediately with your next book. We tend to be closest to the projects we are involved in. If you are involved in another project it won't hurt nearly as much if your previous project is rejected.

I'm not saying it won't be painful – it will, of course, but it won't be as bad if your focus is elsewhere. I promise.

The very worst thing you can do is to down tools and wait to hear the fate of your novel. Carry on writing. The novel you write next may be the novel you sell. It may become a bestseller, it may become a masterpiece; something you will be proud to have written. If you don't write it you will never find out. So it has to be written. You cannot give up. Because when all else is said and done, if you are still writing, there are always possibilities, there is always hope.

Good luck!

Summary of differences

Basically, you are going to need a bigger bottle of wine to drown your sorrows for a novel rejection than you would for a short story rejection!

You are also going to need more courage, but it's worth it. Nothing beats that phone call or email saying "We would like to publish your novel." Nothing beats holding a novel in your hand that has your name on the cover.

Nothing beats the thrill of your first book launch and it's pretty amazing when people tell you they like your novel, particularly when they are not your best friends!

Don't give up on the dream. It's worth it.

Chapter Twenty-four
Tips from the Experts

I hope you have enjoyed this book and found it useful. I hope I have shown you that there are some fundamental differences between writing short stories and novels, but most of all I hope I have helped you to unravel the mysteries of what they are.

Enjoy your novel writing journey, which I don't think ever really finishes. I intend to enjoy mine for many years to come.

Just to conclude, I thought you might like to hear from some other writers who have already made the journey from short story to novel.

I am extremely grateful to these writers who have agreed to share their own experiences of writing long and short fiction. I feel it is always nice to have more than one opinion in a book about writing.

So here they are, in alphabetical order:

Ian Burton, author of three novels, one of which was shortlisted for the Booker Prize, has this to say:

It's all about ideas really. There are short story ideas and there are novel ideas but the important thing is to keep your mind open to all ideas. If an idea walks up to you claiming to be a novel you don't necessarily believe it.

You make it wait, ferment, until you can't help but give it all your attention. With an open mind you avoid getting into the 1,000 word routine and you are then open to everything from flash fiction to saga.

Emma Darwin, author of *The Mathematics of Love* and *A Secret Alchemy*

Characters act as they do because of who they are, and fiction is built of character-in-action. Short fiction usually fleshes out one main change for your main character-in-action and perhaps one or two others, so that, by the end, something important in their internal and/or external life is different. The change may be huge, or tiny: the perfect voice or atmosphere can make even the shortest story resonate.

In long fiction, voice and atmosphere aren't enough, and nor is a single character or three. Each character-in-action has its own story, even thought only bits of the minor stories are visible, where they weave into the main story. And the main change needs to be big – there must be a lot at stake – if it's to drive your narrative all the way to the end. But it takes a chain of smaller changes to keep us turning the pages. So each unit of change – each scene or set of scenes – mustn't be *too* resolved, or leave *too* stable a situation. It needs to leave threads trailing to lead someone on, or trip them up later.

www.emmadarwin.com

Dan Holloway, author of, *Songs from the Other Side of the Wall*

For me the short story has more in common with the

novel than either does with the novella, which, as a form, takes a single idea and pushes it relentlessly almost to breaking. By which I mean that in both the short story and the novel we have a certain freedom to add layers of depth and meaning through tangents and secondary characters and developments upon a central theme. And I don't buy the idea that the short story and the novel are different lenses for the same material, the one compressing the scale, sweep, or time of the other. The short story and the novel have an almost fractal-like relation to each other – they are built in the same way from the same ingredients in the same proportion, and the reader of the short story is left with a mouthful of the same experience as a novel will leave. This makes the short story the perfect tool for precision honing the novel and vice versa.

I hear writers all the time say that the novel is a more forgiving form – that's true only if they're lazy. Likewise I hear people say that a short story doesn't need the rhythms of a novel – which is only true if the writer lacks ambition.

It's true there is a tendency in modern short-story writing to take a scene and play it out, with a limited cast of characters whose pasts and futures may be truncated to fit everything within that unity. And there are great short stories that fit this mould. But it's a fad, not something inherent in the short story. And from Joyce to Tao Lin there are great novels that use the same truncation.

Writers should attempt to excel at both the short story and the novel, and to alternate between the two to ensure their novels never become flabby and their short stories never lose their ambition. And maybe when they've mastered both they can move on to the novella, a different beast entirely, and one I at least find utterly terrifying and absolutely beyond me.'

Bernardine Kennedy, author of contemporary sagas (latest, *Ruby, Harper Collins*) says:

When I was writing short stories and features, moving away from what I called 'the thousand word mind-set' was almost impossible to imagine. I mean, how could anyone write a story of 100,000 words? Surely it would take for ever? How could a story possibly be expanded to fill the pages of an average-sized novel?

But I really wanted to write 'the' novel so I set myself the task, thought of the story I wanted to write, promised my imagination free rein and that was it. I was off.

To make it easier for myself I divided the story into four 'books' and visualised each 'book' as a whole; 25,000 words seemed so much more achievable than 100,000. It worked, and to my amazement a whole book, *Everything Is Not Enough*, emerged and it was accepted straight away. It didn't exactly get easier writing the next one and the next, but at least I knew I could do it.

With a short story, much time is spent trying to craft the tale within the wordage, to take out all the unnecessary adjectives, adverbs and dialogue and weave it to an end when it seems it's barely started.

I love short stories but sometimes as writers we just want to delve deeper into the characters and their settings and this is probably the time to go for it.

It's the time to stop thinking brevity and give your imagination free rein."

www.bernardinekennedy.com

Catherine King, author of romantic historical novels,

latest, *The Orphan Child (Sphere)*

I believe that I am a novelist by nature because when I sit down to write fiction my thoughts tend to roam around a big picture scenario rather than focus on a snapshot. The consequence of this is that I find short stories difficult to tackle as my ideas do not readily fit the shorter format. When a concept forms in my head it usually involves several protagonists each with his or her agenda, in other words it is an outline for a novel.

My fiction is character-driven so if I want to write a shorter piece I have to hook out one of these people and examine his or her strengths and weaknesses before deciding on the plot of the story.

It is easiest for me to write a short story about one of my characters after I have finished a book and know each one very well. Even so, I find the mental gear-change from 'broad brush' approach to hair-line detail hard work.

Having said that, I don't believe that one format is more difficult to write than the other. Each requires its own skill set that must be developed through practice.

www.catherineking.info

Cally Taylor, author of contemporary fiction, (latest, *Home for Christmas, Orion*) says:

Making the transition from short stories to novels was never going to be easy. I write 95 per cent of my short stories in one sitting, normally prompted by a character, a 'what if' situation or a first line/voice that's magically appeared in my head. Often I have no idea how the story will turn out when I pen that first sentence but I'll keep writing until I reach the end. If I'm lucky I've got a finished short story that only requires a bit of tweaking before it's ready to be submitted to an editor or competition. If I'm unlucky I've got the delete button and I've only wasted a couple of hours of my time.

Unlike the average short story which, for me, is about 2,000 words long and takes approximately four hours to write my novels are about 85,000 words long (100,000 words before editing) and take anywhere from four to seven months to complete a first draft. I've got a full time job and write in the evenings and weekends so time is precious and I can't afford to form too close a relationship with the delete button!

When I started writing my first novel, *Heaven Can Wait,* it was a *what if* scenario that prompted me to start writing it – what if a woman died the night before her wedding and refused to go to heaven? With a short story that probably would have been enough for me to start writing but the prospect of writing 100,000 words on a wing and a prayer intimidated me. I needed some road markers along the way. Unlike short stories it was important that I knew, not only the beginning, but also what happened in the middle and at the end. Knowing that much gave me three road markers to journey between: from A (beginning) to B (middle) to C (end) and it was helpful but it wasn't enough. How on earth was I going to fill the gaps between those points?

1) I had a look at the 'Hero's Journey' – the plots of lots of successful films, such as *Star Wars, Four Weddings and a Funeral, Romancing the Stone,* etc., are built on it – and realised that I could adapt some of the stages to use for Lucy, my heroine's, journey.

She was on a quest too – to be reunited with her fiancé – so, with a bit of tweaking, I had a few more road markers to add ('meeting the mentor', 'tests, allies and enemies', 'the ordeal', etc.).

2) I developed subplots. Unlike a short story there's plenty of room for a subplot or two (or three) in a novel. As well as giving Lucy a 'quest' I decided to give her flatmates Brian and Claire quests too and these became the basis for two of the subplots.

3) I thought about Lucy's inner journey. As with a short story the main character should change/develop/ learn something by the end of the story. I spent a lot of time thinking about how Lucy changed as she struggled to obtain her goal. You can go into a lot more detail about a character's inner journey in a novel than you can in a short story.

With my second novel, *Home for Christmas*, I developed points 2 and 3 again but this time I used the three-act structure as a skeleton to hang my plot on and I experimented with switching points of view (the novel is told, alternately, from the POVs of the main characters Beth and Matt).

For me one of the most exciting things about writing short stories was the thrill of not knowing where the story was going and seeing it unfold under my fingers and I need the same kind of buzz when I'm writing a novel. As a result I don't over plot, I just give myself enough road markers that I know where I'm heading and I leave it up to my characters to get me there. Writing a novel is a scary prospect when you've got used to the immediate satisfaction of short stories but the sense of elation when you type 'The End' is second to none.

My top five tips:

1. Decide what your main character's goal is and then

throw as many obstacles at her as you can to stop her reaching her goal. If you want your book to have a happy ending she should overcome each of the obstacles and achieve her goal by the end of the book.

2. Set yourself little targets to motivate yourself – 2,000 words by the end of the week or 10,000 words in a month – and give yourself a little treat when you hit your target. When I was writing *Heaven Can Wait* I bought myself a paperweight for every 25,000 words I wrote. By the end of the first draft I had four very pretty paperweights on the window sill in front of my desk, reminding me of what I'd achieved.

3. Don't keep going back to edit what you've just written. You'll get too bogged down trying to make it perfect and you'll never reach the end of your novel! The most important thing is to get the whole novel written. Most first drafts are rubbish. It's the editing afterwards that turns a draft into a complete, polished book. When you've finished the first draft of your novel set it aside for at least a month before you start editing it. You'll be more removed from it and will spot problems or mistakes that you wouldn't have noticed if you'd started editing immediately after finishing it. It also helps if you read it aloud.

4. You can also learn a lot about writing a novel by studying books by your favourite authors and asking yourself "How did they make that chapter so gripping?" or "Why did that scene make me cry?"

5. Don't be surprised if you get part way through your novel and suddenly all your enthusiasm drains away and

you think your novel is awful. This is perfectly natural and happens to all authors. Give yourself a little bit of a break then continue writing, you will start to believe in your novel again.'

www.callytaylor.co.uk

Jane Wenham-Jones, novelist and author of the brilliant, *Wannabe a Writer?* Latest, *Wannabe a Writer We've Heard Of?* published by *Accent Press*, says:

It is a mistake to assume that because you've had short stories published you'll automatically be able to write a novel – which, I'm afraid, is what I did! At the time of starting my first full-length work I had written around 60 short stories of between 1,000 and 2,000 words each. I therefore took the view that I'd already produced the equivalent of a novel. How difficult could it be to do it again but all in one lump? The answer was very difficult indeed. Writing my first novel was the biggest learning curve of my life and I know I'm not alone. There are best-selling novelists out there who cheerfully admit they cannot pen a decent short story and many a successful short-story writer who has yet to find a publisher for anything longer.

Writing short is an excellent discipline in writing tightly, creating a world in a few words and – if you are writing for magazines – meeting the requirements of the market. All useful stuff but novel writing is something else. You've got to keep the interest going for maybe 50 times as long, think about a proper plot and/or immensely engaging characters, as well as subplots, structure, variety, creating a world that won't just sustain readers through their coffee break but will keep them turning the page every night for a week.

It's a whole different ball game and the best advice I can give is to start out being very aware of that. Read loads of other novels, think about what makes them work and prepare yourself to be in for a long haul. I found I really missed the instant high and endorsement of making a sale or seeing a short story in print fairly regularly. Suddenly there was nothing to open the champagne for! It was just me and the computer screen and a lot of slog. So you need to keep fit, keep cheerful, watch out for Writer's Bottom and keep the momentum up by writing every day – even if you only add a sentence. It won't be easy – nothing one really wants ever is – but when you hold your own book in your hands it will be worth it. Then you can pop the champagne corks again and get slaughtered!

Stella Whitelaw, author of 47 novels and over 300 short stories, as well as lecturer and former Secretary of the Parliamentary Press Gallery at the House of Commons, says:

In the days when editors lunched their writers, Jimmy Low took me to a posh London restaurant. He wanted me to write a serial for D C Thomson.

I declined. "I'm a short story writer," I said. "I can't write a book. It's far too long."

"So think of it as a lot of short stories joined up together, with the same characters and the same setting," said Jimmy Low.

That's how I wrote my first serial which became my first published book.

Forty-seven books later, I still think of a book as a lot of short stories joined up together.

Sally Zigmond, author of *Hope Against Hope*, and numerous prize-winning short stories, says:

I began my writing career with short stories because, at the time, I didn't feel I had the confidence or ability to write a novel. It seemed too daunting a task.

Entering short story competitions and submitting to magazines taught me many valuable lessons; from how to construct a story, how to create characters, etc. to how to set out a manuscript, deal with editors and also (most importantly) take rejection in my stride.

It also became clear that my interests lay mainly with historical fiction. When I felt I was ready to write a novel, I knew exactly what kind of novel I wanted to write. I felt a surge of freedom with the extra scope it gave me and relished the task ahead.

However, short-story writing had taught me how to write 'tight', pace and how to cut unnecessary waffle – the lack of which I find spoils many a promising unpublished manuscript. Therefore I would advise all new writers to have an apprenticeship as a short-story writer and then apply what you've learned to a novel.

Also by Della Galton

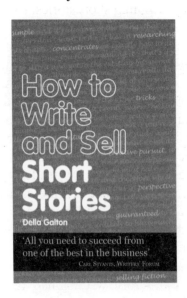

A must-have book for any new writer and a welcome addition to the library of established writers who are hoping to 'up their game'.

Have you ever wondered why your short stories are rejected? What is the secret of selling your work? How do you make sure your characters are memorable, your plots realistic and your twists both satisfying and unpredictable?

Della Galton answers these and many more questions using a format that will already be familiar to writers: What? Why? When? How? Where? and Who?

ISBN 978190637337   £9.99

Helter Skelter

Brought up on a seaside fairground, Vanessa knows all about what a rollercoaster ride life can be. Tragedy forces her to flee but when she discovers that her husband, a property developer, is cheating on her she returns. But the fair has gone, the land, bought by her husband, is now covered by luxury flats.

Going back can be painful but this is just the start of the Helter Skelter for Vanessa. While she feels her life is spiralling ever downwards, there are the strong arms of a passion from her past to catch her at the end.

ISBN 9781905170971   £6.99

DELLA GALTON

Passing Shadows

Passing Shadows

How do you choose between friendship and love?
Maggie faces an impossible dilemma when she discovers
that Finn, the man she loves, is also the father of her best
friend's child. Should Maggie betray her best friend, who
never wanted him to know? Or lie to Finn, the first man
she's ever trusted enough to love? The decision is
complicated by the shadows of her past.

ISBN 9781905170234 £6.99

Also from Accent Press

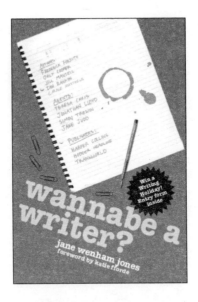

Wannabe a Writer?
Jane Wenham-Jones

Wannabe a Writer? This hilarious, informative guide to getting into print, is a must-have for anyone who's ever thought they've got a book in them.

Drawing on her own experiences as a novelist and journalist, **Writing Magazine's** agony aunt **Jane Wenham-Jones** takes you through the minefield of the writing process, giving advice on everything from how to avoid Writers' Bottom to what to wear to your launch party.

Including hot tips from authors, agents and publishers at the sharp end of the industry, **Wannabe a Writer?** tells you everything you ever wanted to know about the book world - and a few things you didn't...

ISBN 9781905170814   £9.99

Accent Press Ltd

Please visit our website
www.accentpress.co.uk
for our latest title information,
to write reviews and
leave feedback.

We'd love to hear from you!